ALSO BY ANDREW SULLIVAN

Virtually Normal:
An Argument About Homosexuality

EDITOR

Same-Sex Marriage: Pro and Con

LOVE UNDETECTABLE

LOVE UNDETECTABLE

Notes on Friendship, Sex, and Survival

Andrew Sullivan

ALFRED A. KNOPF NEW YORK 1999

THIS IS A BORZOI BOOK
PUBLISHED BY ALFRED A. KNOPF, INC.

www.randomhouse.com

Owing to a limitation of space, all acknowledgments for
permission to reprint previously published material
may be found on page 256.

Library of Congress Cataloging-in-Publication Data
Sullivan, Andrew
Love undetectable : notes on friendship, sex, and survival /
Andrew Sullivan. — 1st ed.
p.   cm.
ISBN 0-679-45119-6 (alk. paper)
1. Gay men—United States—Social conditions.
2. Gay men—United States—Sexual behavior.
3. AIDS (Disease)—Patients—United States.
4. HIV infections—Patients—United States.
5. Homosexuality—United States—Public opinion.
6. Public opinion—United States. I. Title.
HQ76.3.U5S85   1998
305.38'9664'0973—dc21   98-13502   CIP

Manufactured in the United States of America
Published October 7, 1998
Second Printing, March 1999

Because I do not hope to know again
The infirm glory of the positive hour . . .
—T. S. Eliot, *Ash-Wednesday*

CONTENTS

THESE THREE ESSAYS are both connected and unconnected, a fact perhaps best explained by the following chronology. When I first sat down to write a book about friendship, I realized that I could not begin it without first writing about the death of one of my closest friends, and the puzzling context of new hope which surrounded it. From that piece of writing came an essay, "When Plagues End," published on November 11, 1996, in the *New York Times Magazine*. In the way these things sometimes develop, I realized then that there was more to say about the experience of survival, and embarked on expanding "When Plagues End" into a broader essay, postponing for a while the work on friendship. And then in the process of writing, it occurred to me that, in fact, the two subjects were, after all, inseparable. So both "When Plagues End" and "If Love Were All" emerged as different answers to the same questions, different responses to the same period in my life, different parts, I hope, of the same book.

As for "Virtually Abnormal," it was clear to me that in the post-AIDS political debate about homosexuality, something apolitical and unavoidable was re-emerging. And that was the psychological debate about the origins of homosexuality itself. I carefully avoided the issue in my first book, *Virtually Normal*, because I considered it irrelevant to a political discussion, and still do. It seems to me that the only relevant political issue with regard to the nature of homosexuality in a free society is whether it is honestly experienced by adult citizens as involuntary, whatever its genesis. But the question of where homosexuality comes from is still a fascinating one, and one that seemed to me increasingly central, if somewhat taboo, in the burgeoning discussion about sex, marriage, and homosexual relationships. It was also a question that, until the experience of the plague years, had always unnerved me. With the new possibility of survival, I wanted to test my nerve.

I hope these essays can be read separately, and make sense separately, but I hope also that their common context makes some sort of unifying sense. It is a context of extremity, and the questions such an experience, even as it recedes, continues to ask.

I am grateful to Adam Moss of the *New York Times Magazine,* who guided the first draft of "When Plagues End." (About a third of the first essay is adapted from that article. One small passage about the AIDS quilt also appeared first in *The New Republic.*) And I would like to thank Sarah Chalfant, Alane Mason, Joe Landau, Joe James, Jeff Hoover, Robert Cameron, Teresa Lynch, Barney McManigal, Wendy Kohn, Evan Wolfson, Patrick Giles, Steve Daigneault, Christopher Devron, S.J., John Dugdale, Greg Scott, Liz Young, Andrew Wylie, Naomi Wolf, Chris Keller, and Roy Tsao for reading drafts, offering encouragement, and giving invaluable suggestions along the way. My colleagues on the Beyond Queer list server also kept me stimulated and alert throughout the writing of this book, and generated discussions which informed its contents. My doctors, Jerry Groopman, Tim Price, and Betty-Ann Ottinger, kept me on an even keel throughout. The support of my editor, Jane Garrett, and my agents, Andrew Wylie and Sarah Chalfant, was vital to the book's existence. And Chris Grasso helped me not only improve the manuscript immeasurably but also understand why no account of friendship in words can approximate the beauty of it in action.

All the undetected errors, of course, remain my own.

Washington, D.C., June 1998

LOVE UNDETECTABLE

1. WHEN PLAGUES END

> The sense of what is real . . . the thought
> if after all it should prove unreal . . .
> —Walt Whitman, *Leaves of Grass*

FIRST, THE RESISTANCE to memory.

I arrived late at the hospital, fresh off the plane. It was around 8:30 and there was no light on in my friend Patrick's apartment, so I went straight to the intensive care unit. When I arrived, my friend Chris's eyes were a reddened blear of fright, the hospital mask slipped down under his chin. I went into the room. When I first caught sight of Pat, he was lying on his back, his body contorted so his neck twisted away and his arms splayed out, his hands palm upward, showing the intravenous tubes into his wrists. Blood mingled with sweat in the creases of his neck, his chest heaving up and down grotesquely with the pumping of the respirator, a huge plastic tube forced down his throat. His cold feet poked out from under the bedspread, as if separate from the rest of his body.

The week before, celebrating his thirty-first birthday in his hometown on the Gulf Coast of Florida, we had swum together in the dark, warm space he had already decided would one day contain his ashes. It was clear that he had known something was about to happen. One afternoon on the beach, he had gotten up to take a walk with his newly acquired beagle, and had glanced back at me a second before he left. All I can say is that, somehow, the glance conveyed a complete sense of finality, the subtlest but clearest sign that it was, as far as he was concerned, over.

Within three days, a massive fungal infection overtook his lungs, and at midnight, the vital signs began to plummet.

I remember walking slowly back to the intensive care room when a sudden rush of people moved backwards out of the room. His brother motioned to the rest of us to run, and we sped toward him. Pat's heart had stopped beating and after one attempt to restart it, we surrounded him and prayed: his mother and father and three brothers, his boyfriend, ex-boyfriend and a handful of close friends. When the priest arrived, each of us received communion. I remember I slumped back against the wall at the moment of his dying, reaching out for all the consolation I had been used to reaching for—the knowledge that the worst was yet to come, the memory of pain survived in the past—but since it was happening now, and now had never felt so unavoidable, no relief was possible.

Perhaps this is why so many of us have found it hard to accept that this ordeal may be over. Because it means we may now be required to relent from our clenching against the future and remember the past.

IF I COULD PINPOINT a moment when the reality sunk in for me, it was a summer evening in 1996. I was at the July 30 meeting of something called the Treatment Action Group, an AIDS activist organization, in Manhattan. In its heyday, in the early 1990s, this group had lived and breathed a hard-edged skepticism. They were, after all, the no-nonsense successors to the AIDS action group, ACT UP. But as soon as I arrived—for a meeting to discuss the data presented at a recent A I D S conference—I could sense something had changed. Even at eight o'clock, there was a big crowd—much larger, one of the organizers told me, than the regular meetings. In the middle sat David Ho, a pioneering A I D S researcher, and Marty Markowitz, the doctor who had presided over some of the earliest clinical trials of the new "combination therapy" for H I V infection. As the crowd stared at them and they stared nervously back, the two scientists interspersed their whispers to one another with the occasional, gleeful smile.

The meeting began with a blur of data. Ho and Markowitz detailed again what had already hit the headlines: how, in some trials of patients taking the new protease inhibitors used in combination with older A I D S drugs, the amount of virus in the bloodstream had been reduced on average by between a hundred- and a thousand-fold. Within a few weeks of treatment with the new drugs, they elaborated, levels of up to six million viral particles in a milliliter of a patient's blood had been reduced to below four hundred in most cases. That is, no virus could be found on the most sophisticated tests available. And, so far, the results had lasted.

When Ho finished speaking, there was, at first, a numbed silence. And then the questions followed, like firecrackers of denial. How long did it take for the virus to clear from the bloodstream? What about the virus still hiding in the brain or the testes? What could be done for the people who weren't responding to the new drugs? Was there resistance to the new therapy? Could a new, even more lethal viral strain be leaking out into the population? The answers that came from Ho and Markowitz were just as insistent. No, this was not a "cure." But the disappearance of the virus in the bloodstream was beyond the expectations of even the most optimistic of researchers. It was likely that there would be some impact on the virus—although less profound—in the brain or testes, and new drugs were able to reach those areas better. And since the impact of the drugs was so powerful, it was hard for resistance to develop because resistance is what happens when the virus mutates in the presence of the drugs—and *there was no virus detectable in the presence of the drugs.*

The crowd palpably adjusted itself; and a few rusty office chairs squeaked. These were the hard-core skeptics, I remember thinking to myself, and even they couldn't disguise what was going through their minds. There were caveats, of course. The latest drugs were very new, and large studies had yet to be done. There was already clinical evidence that a small minority of patients, especially those in late-stage disease, were not responding as well to the new drugs and were experiencing a "breakout" of the virus after a few weeks or months. Although some people's immune systems seemed to recover, others' seemed damaged for good. The long-term toxicity of the drugs themselves—their impact on the liver and heart, for example—could mean that patients might stage a miraculous recovery at the start, only to die from the effects of treatment in later life. And the drugs themselves were often debilitating. After testing positive in 1993, I had been on combination therapy ever since. When I added the protease inhibitors in March of 1996, the nausea, diarrhea, and constant fatigue had been overwhelming.

But I remember that meeting all too vividly now, and the

simple, unavoidable future it presaged. The next day, in a friend's apartment, I spoke the words I never believed I would speak in my lifetime. "It's over," I said. "Believe me. It's over."

MOST OFFICIAL STATEMENTS about the disease, of course—the statements by responsible scientists, by AIDS activist organizations, by doctors—do not concede that the plague is at an end. And, in one vital sense, obviously it's not. In the time it takes you to read this sentence, someone somewhere will be infected with HIV. Worldwide, the numbers affected jump daily—some 30 million human beings at the latest estimate. Almost all of these people—and a real minority in America—will not be able to have access to the treatments now available. And many, many of these people will still die. Nothing I am saying here is meant to deny that fact, or to mitigate its awfulness. I am not saying here (nor would I ever say) that some lives are worth more than others, or that some lives are worth more attention than others. To speak of the experience of some is not to deny the experience of others or to deny its importance. But it is not illegitimate to speak of what you know, while conceding a large part of what you do not know. And there is a speciousness to the idea that what is true is somehow untrue because it isn't everything.

So I do not apologize for the following sentence. It is true—and truer now than it was when it was first spoken, and truer now than even six months ago—that something profound in the history of AIDS has occurred these last two years. The power of the new treatments and the even greater power of those now in the pipeline are such that a diagnosis of HIV infection in the West is not just different in degree today than, say, in 1994. For those who can get medical care, the diagnosis is quite different in kind. It no longer signifies death. It merely signifies illness.

This is a shift as immense as it is difficult to grasp. So let me make what I think is more than a semantic point: a plague is not the same thing as a disease. It is possible, for example, for a plague to end, while a disease continues. A plague is something that cannot be controlled, something with a capacity to spread exponentially out of its borders, something that kills and devastates with democratic impunity, something that robs human beings of the ability to respond in any practical way. Disease, in contrast, is generally diagnosable and treatable, with varying degrees of success; it occurs at a steady or predictable rate; it counts its progress through the human population one person, and often centuries, at a time. Plague, on the other hand, cannot be cured, and it never affects one person. It affects many, and at once, and swiftly. And by its very communal nature, by its unpredictability and by its devastation, plague asks questions disease often doesn't. Disease is experienced; plague is spread. Disease is always with us; plagues come and go. And some time toward the end of the millennium in America, the plague of AIDS went.

You could see it in the papers. Almost overnight, toward the end of 1996, the obituary pages in the gay press began to dwindle. Soon after, the official statistics followed. Within a year, AIDS deaths had plummeted 60 percent in

California, 44 percent across the country as a whole. In time, it was shown that triple combination therapy in patients who had never taken drugs before kept close to 90 percent of them at undetectable levels of virus for two full years. Optimism about actually ridding the body completely of virus dissipated; what had at one point been conceivable after two years stretched to three and then longer. But even for those who had developed resistance to one or more drugs, the future seemed tangibly brighter. New, more powerful treatments were fast coming onstream, month after month. What had once been a handful of treatment options grew to over twenty. In trials, the next generation of AZT packed a punch ten times as powerful as its original; and new, more focused forms of protease inhibitor carried with them even greater promise. It was still taboo, of course, to mention this hope—for fear it might encourage a return to unsafe sex and a new outburst of promiscuity. But, after a while, the numbers began to speak for themselves.

It remains true, however, that anyone who even understood the minimal amount of the science could have predicted these figures as early as 1995. By that steamy summer night in 1996, the implications were unavoidable, and you could sense it in the air. After the meeting, as we spilled out into the street, a slightly heady feeling wafted over the crowd. A few groups headed off for a late dinner, others to take their protease drugs quickly on an empty stomach, others still to bed. It was after ten o'clock, and I remember wandering aimlessly into a nearby bar, where late-evening men in suits gazed up at muscle-boy videos, their tired faces and occasional cruising glances a weirdly comforting return to normality. But as I checked my notebook at the door and returned to the bar to order a drink, the phrase a longtime AIDS activist had spoken to me earlier that day began to reverberate in my mind. He'd been talking about the sense of purpose and destiny he had once felt as part of his diagnosis. "It must be hard to find out you're positive now," he had said, darkly. "It's like you really missed the party."

AT SIX O'CLOCK in the morning in Manhattan's Roseland Ballroom, the crowds were still thick. I'd arrived four hours earlier, after a failed attempt to sleep beforehand. A chaotic throng of men crammed the downstairs lobby, attempting to check coats. There were no lines as such, merely a subterranean, almost stationary mosh pit, stiflingly hot, full of inflated muscular bodies, glacially drifting toward the coat-check windows. This was, for some, the high point of the year's gay male social calendar. It's called the Black Party, one of a series of theme parties held year-round by a large, informal group of affluent, mainly white, gay men and several thousand admirers. It's part of what's been dubbed the "circuit," a series of vast, drug-enhanced dance parties held in various cities across the country, and now a resilient, if marginal, feature of an emergent post-AIDS gay urban "lifestyle."

Until the late 1990s, almost nothing had been written in the mainstream media about these parties, except when they had jutted their way into controversy. A new circuit party, called "Cherry Jubilee," in Washington, D.C., incurred the wrath of Congressman Robert Dornan for tolerating drug use in a federal building leased for the event. The annual Morning Party in August in Fire Island, held to raise money for Gay Men's Health Crisis in New York, was criticized on similar grounds by many in the gay world itself. But slowly, the proliferation of these events (they numbered at least two a month in cities as diverse as Miami and Pittsburgh) became impossible to ignore, and the secrecy that once shrouded them turned into an increasingly raucous debate on the front pages of newspapers across the country. Despite representing a tiny sub-subculture and dwarfed, for example, by the explosion of gay religion and spirituality in the same period, the parties seemed to symbolize something larger: the question of whether, as AIDS receded, gay men were prepared to choose further integration, or were poised to leap into another spasm of libidinal pathology.

The Black Party, like all such events, was made possible by a variety of chemicals: steroids, which began as therapy for wasting men with AIDS, and became a means to perpetuate still further the cult of bodybuilding; and psychotherapeutic designer drugs, primarily Ecstasy, ketamine (or "Special K"), and "crystal meth." The whole place, without this knowledge, could be taken for a mass of men in superb shape, merely enjoying an opportunity to let off steam. But underneath, there was an air of strain, of sexual danger translated into sexual objectification, the unspoken withering of the human body transformed into a reassuring inflation of muscular body mass.

I had never known these events in their heyday, in the

late 1970s and early 1980s. Begun in a legendary disco in Manhattan, the Saint, they had mesmerized an entire generation of homosexual urbanites. I was taken to one in the mid-1980s, as the plague had begun to descend, but even then, its effects were hard to determine. What you saw was an oasis of astonishing masculine beauty, of a kind our society never self-consciously displays in the open. I remember feeling at first a gasp of disbelief, a sense that, finally, I was surrounded by visions that had once only existed in my head. These people were not boys, they were men. And they were not merely men, they were men in the deepest visible sense of that word, men whose muscular power flickered in the shadows, men whose close sweat and buzzed hair and predatory posturing intimated almost a parody of the masculine, men whose self-conscious sexuality set them apart from the heterosexual world—and indeed from the homosexual world outside the hallowed precepts of this space. What would the guardians of reality think, I remember asking myself, if they could see this now, see this display of unapologetic masculinity, and understand that it was homosexual?

The critics of these events have predictably lambasted this glorification of the masculine. They have seen in it an echo of the gender oppression directed by straight men against gay men and lesbians and heterosexual women, an appropriation by homosexuals of the very male supremacy that stigmatizes and marginalizes them. And indeed, in the darkness of that night there was an unmistakably Darwinian element to the whole exercise. While the slim and effeminate hovered at the margins, the center of the dance floor and the stage areas were dedicated to the most male archetypes, their muscles and arrogance like a magnet of self-contempt for the rest. But at the same time, it was hard also not to be struck, as I was the first time I saw it, by a genuine, brazen act of cultural defiance, a spectacle designed not only to exclude but to reclaim a gender, the ultimate response to a heterosexual order that denies gay men the masculinity that is also their own.

And much of it was not merely playacting. To be sure, if you looked around, you saw an efflorescence of masculine symbolism that was as strained as it was crude. Thick torsos, bull necks, and ribbed abdominals were draped with the paraphernalia of the archetype: leather, sports clothes, sneakers, tank tops, tattoos. But behind it, a more convincing affect: beyond the dancing and socializing, a kind of circling, silent interaction, a drifting, almost menacing, courtship of male brevity and concision. It was raw male sexuality distilled, of a kind that unites straight and gay men and separates them from women: without emotion, without knowledge, without apparent weakness, armored with testosterone and an almost marblelike hardness of touch.

There was a numbness to it, as well. The first few times I went to these events, I made an elementary mistake of trying to engage my fellow partiers, of trying to catch their eyes or strike up conversation. But they were anesthetized, almost as if this display was only possible by distancing themselves from their mental being, pushing themselves into a drug-induced distance from their minds and others', turning their bodies into images in a catalogue whose pages they turned, in a bored, fitful trance.

And as the night stretched into morning, and as the drugs reached their peak in the bloodstream of these masses, the escape became more complete, the otherness more perfect, the paradox of reclaiming their selves more intense as the outside world got up, made coffee, and busied itself about the day. I remember once leaving one of these parties at 11:30 in the morning, a dark, cavernous blur of flesh and body still imprinted on my mind when, in an instant, we were thrust out onto the streets of Manhattan, unthinking strangers walking briskly past in the bright whiteness of a cloudy morning. None of this, I felt, cared for us; none of it even knew of us. Which was both a thoroughly depressing and energizing thought.

What these events really were not about, whatever their critics have claimed, was sex. And as circuit parties intensified in frequency and numbers in the 1990s, this became more, not less, the case. When people feared that the ebbing of AIDS would lead to a new burst of promiscuity, to a return to the 1970s in some mindless celebration of old times, they were, it turns out, only half right. Although some bathhouses revived, their centrality to gay life all but disappeared. What replaced sex was the idea of sex; and what replaced promiscuity was the idea of promiscuity, masked, in the burgeoning numbers of circuit parties around the country, by the ecstatic high of drug-enhanced dance music. These were not merely mass celebrations on the dawn of a new era; they were raves built upon the need for amnesia.

They were, of course, built on drugs. And the kind of drugs was as revealing as the fact of them: Ecstasy, a substance that instantly simulated an intimacy so many men found almost impossible to achieve, and an exhilaration they could not otherwise allow themselves to feel; ketamine, a powder that tipped them into an oblivion a part of them inwardly craved; crystal meth, a substance that gave them an endurance and power they hadn't yet been able to attain for real; and anabolic steroids—literally, injected masculinity—providing an illusion of male self-confidence where far too little of it existed for real. These drugs are illusions—pathetic, debilitating—and also telling illusions. They are rightly seen as the antithesis of the new era of responsibility and maturity the end of AIDS actually promised. But they are also, perhaps, merely the cheapest version of such an era, lasting hours, not decades, and bought with money, not life.

In the circuit parties you see perhaps the double-edged nature of a segment of gay male sexuality as clearly as anywhere else: the physical shallowness and emotional cowardice, the cult of youth, and the longing for masculinity; but also the desperate need for belonging, for support and reassurance, above all for intimacy, for a world which can offer gay men, if only they could seize it, the chance for the emotional reality which this spectacle of alienation merely intimated and postponed.

As the early morning stretched on, my friends and I stood in the recess of a back bar as the parade of bodies passed relentlessly by. Some of them glided past, intent on some imminent conquest; others stumbled toward me, eyes glazed, bodies stooped in a kind of morbid stupor, staring at the floor or into space; others still stood in corners, chatting, socializing, their arms draped around each other, a banal familiarity belying the truly bizarre scene around them. Beyond, a mass of men danced the early morning through, strobe lights occasionally glinting off the assorted deltoids, traps, lats, and other muscle groups. At the party's peak—around 7 a.m.—there must have been around six thousand men in the room, some parading on a distant stage, others locked in a cluster of rotating pectoral muscles, embracing each other in a drug-induced emotional high. And then the habitual climax, the sound of the Black Party's signature song, "Left to My Own Devices," a gay elegy of longing and detachment, descended on the scene:

> *I could leave you,*
> *Say Goodbye.*
> *I could love you,*
> *If I tried.*
> *And I could.*
> *And left to my own devices, I probably would.*

And as the music pounded, and the men swarmed closer together, and the posture of maleness and intimacy melded into one hazy blur of movement, I found myself moving quietly away. For a group of men who had just witnessed a scale of loss normally visited only upon war generations, it was a curious spectacle. For some, I'm sure, the drugs helped release emotions they could hardly address alone or sober; for others, the ritual was a way of defying their own infections, their sense of fragility or guilt at survival. For others still, including myself, it was a conflicting puzzle of impulses. The need to find some solidarity among the loss, to assert some crazed physicality against the threat of sickness, to release some of the toxins built up over a decade of constant stress. Beyond everything, the desire to banish the memories that will not be banished, to shuck off—if only till the morning— the maturity that plague had brutally imposed.

But even so, I couldn't be among them. It was too much to experience—at least, not together.

I TALK ABOUT THIS as a quintessentially homosexual experience, not because AIDS is a quintessentially homosexual experience. Across the world, it has affected far, far more heterosexuals than homosexuals; in America, it has culled almost as many people by intravenous drug use. And its impact has been probably as profound on many of the heterosexual family members and friends as on the gay men at ground zero of the epidemic. But, at the same time, AIDS was and is inextricable from the homosexual question in the psyche of America, because it struck homosexuals first and, from then on, became unalterably woven into the deeper and older question of homosexual integration. That, I think, was truer five years ago than today—but it is still largely true.

And in so many ways, in retrospect, it was a bizarre turn of events. In the past, plagues were often marked by their lack of discrimination, by the way in which they laid low vast swaths of the population, with little regard for station, or wealth, or gender, or religion. But AIDS was different. It immediately presented as much a political as a public health problem. Before homosexuals had even been acknowledged as a significant presence in American life, they were suddenly at the heart of a health crisis as profound as any in modern American history. It was always possible, of course, that with such a lack of social preparation America would have responded the way many Latin American and Asian countries responded—with almost complete silence and denial—or that the gay world itself would have collapsed under the strain of its own immolation. But despite an early, culpable fumble, you can see now that, over the long run, something somewhat different happened. AIDS compelled a form of social integration that might never have taken place without its onslaught. Forced to choose between complete abandonment of the homosexual subculture and an awkward first encounter, America, for the most part, chose the latter. A small step, perhaps, but an enormous catalyst in the continuing renegotiation of the gay-straight social contract.

And an enormous shift in our understanding of homosexuality itself. Too much has been made of the analogy between AIDS and the Jewish Holocaust, and they are, indeed, deeply distinct phenomena. One was an act of calculated human evil, obliterating by design a race from the center of Europe. The other is a natural calamity, singling out a group of despised outsiders by a freak of nature, a subculture of sexual compulsion, and a disease that remained asymptomatic long enough to wipe out thousands before anyone knew what was happening. But insofar as each event changed dramatically the way a minority group was viewed by the world, the two have eerie parallels.

The hostility to homosexuals, after all, has far more in common with anti-Semitism than it does with racism.

Homosexuals, like Jews, are not, in the psychology of group hatred, despised because they are deemed to be weak or inferior, but precisely because they are neither. Both Jews and homosexuals appear in the hater's mind as small, cliquish, and very powerful groups, antipathetic to majority values, harboring secret contempt for the rest of society, and sustaining a ghetto code of secrecy and disguise. Even the details resonate. The old libel against Jews—that they would drink the blood of Christian children—has an echo today in the bigot's insistence that he has nothing against homosexuals per se, but doesn't want them allowed near his kids. The notion that any mark of equality granted to each group is immediately a "special" equality given to a specially influential group, a "special right" awarded to a privileged and self-regarding sect, is another striking parallel. The loathing of each group is also closely linked to fear, and the fear is fanned, in many ways, by the distortion of a particular strain in Christian theology.

But that fear was abated, in both cases, by extraordinary, contingent historic events. What the Holocaust did to the structure of anti-Semitism was many things, but, in one, hideous swoop, it helped destroy the myth that Jews were somehow all powerful. The mounds of bodies, the piles of artifacts, the hideous physical torture that the Jews of Europe suffered were not exactly indicators of power. Out of that powerlessness, of course, came a new form of power, in the shape of achieved Zionism. But the image of Jewish victimhood seared by mass murder into the Western consciousness was seared indelibly—and it remains one of the strongest weapons against the canards of anti-Semitism today.

Similarly, if on a far smaller and more tentative scale, AIDS dramatically altered the cultural strength of homophobia. By visiting young death upon so many, it ripped apart the notion of subterranean inviolability that forms such a powerful part of the fear of homosexuals. It need not have happened that way, of course. The notion that AIDS was divine punishment might have gained far wider consensus. The possibility of a mass quarantine, of forced ghettoization, of intensified stigma could have turned the epidemic into a terrifying reinforcement of homosexual otherness. But as tens of thousands of sons and uncles and brothers and fathers wasted away in the heart of America, something somewhat different happened. The image of secretive power that homosexuals allegedly held melted into a surprised form of shock and empathy. For some the old hatreds endured, of course, but for others an unsought-for and subtle transformation began to take shape. What had once been a strong fear of homosexual difference, disguising mostly silent awareness of homosexual humanity, became reversed. The humanity slowly trumped the difference. Death, it turned out, was a powerfully universalizing experience. Suddenly, acquiescence in gay baiting and gay bashing became, even in its strongholds, something inappropriate at a moment of tragedy. The victimization of gay men by a disease ironically undercut their victimization by a culture. There was no longer a need to kick them when they were already down.

I think this helps explain the change in the American psyche these last ten years from one of fearful stigmatization to one of awkward, fitful acquiescence. And it's revealing that the same thing did not really happen to the many other victims of the plague. With inner-city blacks and Latinos, with intravenous drug users, there was no similar cultural transformation, no acceleration of social change. And that was because, with these groups, there had never been a myth of power. They had always been, in the majority psyche, a series of unknowable victims. AIDS merely perpetuated what was already understood and, in some ways, intensified it. With gay men, in contrast, a social revolution had been initiated. From being invisible, they were now unavoidable, from being powerful subversives, they were now dying sons.

AIDS, then, was an integrator. If the virus separated, death integrated. But there was a twist to this tale. As the straight world found itself at a moment of awkward reconciliation, the gay world discovered something else entirely. At a time when gay integration with heterosexual life had never been so necessary or profound, the experience of AIDS as a homosexual experience created bonds and loyalties and solidarities that homosexuals had never experienced before. As it forced gay men out into the world, it also paradoxically intensified the bonds among them; as it accelerated an integration, it forged an even deeper separation. The old question of assimilation-versus-separatism became strangely moot. Now, both were happening at once—and feeding off the same psychological roots.

I remember the first time I used the word "we" in reference to gay men in print. It was in an article I was writing as I witnessed my first AIDS death—a stranger I had volunteered to help out in his final months. He was thirty-two years old when I got to know him, back in 1990. Without AIDS, we would never have met, and the experience changed my sense of gay identity for good. Before then, although I had carefully denied it, I had quietly distanced myself from much of what I thought of as "gay culture." Tom helped to change this. He was the stereotype in so many ways—the 1970s mustache, the Alcoholics Anonymous theology, the Miss America Beauty Pageant fan, the college swim coach. But he was also dying. Under his thick pebble glasses, his skin was clammy and pale. His apartment smelled of Maxwell House coffee and disinfectant and the gray liquid that was his constant, uncontrollable diarrhea. As he lay down on the couch in the afternoons watching soap operas, with a plastic bedpan under his hips, he would spew the stuff out involuntarily—and with no warning, while he talked or meandered or merely slept. I remember one day lying down on top of him to restrain him as his brittle, burning body shook uncontrollably with the convulsions of fever. I had never done such a thing to a grown man before—and as I did, the defenses I had put up between us, the categories that until then had helped me make sense of my life and his, these defenses began to crumble into something more like solidarity.

For others, the shift was more dramatic. Their own incipient deaths unleashed the unfiltered rage of the late 1980s, as decades of euphemism and self-loathing exploded into one dark, memorable flash of activism. The fire behind ACT UP and the engine of its energy was of its very nature so combustible that it soon fizzled. But its articulation of a

common identity—the unsustainable starkness of its definition of homosexuality—left a residue behind.

And the pull of this identity I began more instinctively to
understand. Suddenly, it seemed, as my twenties merged
into my thirties, everyone had it. Faces you had gotten used
to seeing in the gym kept turning up on the obit pages. New
friends took you aside to tell you they had just tested positive. Old flames suddenly were absent from the bars. I
remember thinking they should have devised a new term
for something that was happening to me with increasing
frequency: I would be walking along a street and see an old
man coming toward me whom I vaguely recognized. And
then I'd realize that it wasn't an old man; it was someone
I knew who had just gone through some bout of pneumonia, or some intestinal parasite. Like Scott, a soldier I'd gotten to know in the late 1980s as a 200-pound, six-foot,
blue-eyed, blond-haired bundle of energy. During the gays-
in-the-military affair, I'd urged him to come out to his commanders and troops, sure that the new president would
protect him. He told me I had to be out of my mind and, of
course, as it turned out, I was. And then, a few weeks later,
he bumped into me on the street and confided the real reason he didn't want to confront anyone. He was HIV-positive
and needed the army's support. He told me with genuine
anguish, as if the knowledge of his disease demanded a
courage his commanders would also have punished.

And then, a mere year later, I saw him one day literally with a cane, his spirit completely broken, his body
shrunk to 140 pounds, his breath gone after the short-
est walk, his eyes welling with the bitterness of physical

pain and isolation. His lover of several years somehow endured the ordeal, nursing him every inch of the way, until Scott became a 90-pound skeletal wreck, unable to walk, his hair weak and gray and glassy, his eyes sunken miserably into a scaly face. Scott's family had not been particularly supportive. And after Scott died, his lover told me that his last words had been, "Tell my mother I hate her."

I remember that when I would tell my straight friends about these things, or my work colleagues, or my family, they tried hard to sympathize. But something didn't compute. It was as if they sensed that the experience was slowly and profoundly alienating me from them and that it was more than just a cultural difference. The awareness of the deaths of one's peers, and the sadness they evoke, and the pain you are forced to witness—not just the physical pain but all the psychological fear and shame that AIDS unleashed—all this was slowly building a kind of solidarity that gradually ruled my straight friends out of the most meaningful part of my life. There comes a point at which the experience goes so deep that it becomes almost futile to communicate it. And as you tell them less and less and experience more and more, you find yourself gravitating to the people who have experienced it as well, the ones who know instinctively, the people to whom you do not have to explain.

For a long time, I never broke down or cried about any of the experiences of the plague years—the dozens of acquaintances who had died, the handful of friends I had mourned or resisted mourning, the sudden flashes of panic at the thought of my own mortality. But late one night, I caught sight of Senator Bob Kerrey on *Nightline*.

He was speaking, haltingly, of his relationship with Lewis B. Puller Jr., the paralyzed Vietnam veteran who had survived the war, only ultimately to succumb to depression, alcoholism, and finally, suicide. There was in Kerrey's bitter, poignant farewell a sense that only he and a few others would fully understand Puller's anguish. Kerrey grasped, because he had experienced, what it was to face extreme danger, and witness in the most graphic way possible the death of his closest friends and colleagues, only to come home and find those experiences denied or ignored or simply not understood. And as he spoke, I felt something break inside me. He knew, in Mark Helprin's beautiful words in his novel *A Soldier of the Great War,* what gay men, in a subtler and quieter way have also learned, that "the war was still in him, and it would be in him for a long time to come, for soldiers who have been bloodied are soldiers forever. They never fit in . . . That they cannot forget, that they do not forget, that they will never allow themselves to heal completely, is their way of expressing their love for friends who have perished. And they will not change because they have become what they have become to keep the fallen alive."

By the time the agony abated, some five times as many young Americans had died of AIDS as died in the entire Vietnam War.

WHAT I AM ABOUT TO SAY will seem to some an absurdity, to others a self-delusion, to still others, perhaps, a piece of morbid self-aggrandizement. It is hard to write about faith without invoking one of these responses. Nevertheless, I know, insofar as I can know anything, that what happened to me in the months during and after my seroconversion really did happen to me. And it meant something. Something I am still trying to explicate and understand.

I came back from dinner one early-summer Sunday night, and within an hour felt suddenly sick. The fevers started right away, and with such immediacy and with so little warning that I immediately suspected food poisoning. By one in the morning, my fever had risen to 104, and my body shook. I called my doctor. No response. The fever then subsided, as quickly as it began. Soaked in sweat, and shuddering with the ebb of a chill, I took a warm shower and changed my clothes. But as I went back to bed the fever started again, rising ominously, this time to 105, whiplashing my body, making me feel like an animal thrashed around by the neck by a predator desperately trying to break its spine. It went on for two days, a relentless, hostile, virulent thrashing, a deep, spiking fever that I had never experienced before and had no idea how to confront. It was a new level of illness I could sense, something my body and mind had never encountered before, something my memory had no reference for, something I intuitively knew was beyond and above my mental and physical control. Nevertheless, in the moments when the fever seized me most violently, I could feel my body fighting back, resisting whatever it was that had me by the throat. Until one night, when I crawled out of bed to get to the bathroom, terrified that this time the fever might truly spike into the emergency zone, trying to cover myself in cold water, to cool myself down. And as I walked toward the bathroom, my legs suddenly gave way beneath me, something deep inside my body snapping, as if in some internal battle of wills my body had finally succumbed to whatever was invading it.

From then on, the fevers spiked at lower and lower levels, fading out into a low-level malaise, and I lay in bed for days, wondering what kind of flu this was, slowly coming back into territory my body seemed to recognize and master. And it was on one of those afternoons, as I lay in bed, watching a television movie, that I felt something change around me. I know where it was on the wall, a space that had no shape, a presence that had no form, something that I can only call an intensification of light and space. And as I lay there, I felt it intensify, and I felt it announce itself. For a moment, I thought the fever had made me hallucinate, but I felt my skin and it was cool. My eyes rested quietly in their sockets, my mouth was moist, my pulse normal. The television flickered in front of me, but my mind was dead to it. And this presence, although it had no shape and spoke no words, nevertheless commanded a tone, a tone at once admonitory and intimate, firm and solid but of a kindness I could not even allow myself to feel. It was, although soundless, a tone of voice, a tone of voice in a space of light, an insistent, minatory, so-personal voice. And although I couldn't hear it, I knew it; and it knew me.

And then it was no longer there. The space dissipated, the tone seeped away, the intensity ebbed. The wall became the wall again, the air became the air, the bed held my body with a tangible familiarity. I looked at the clock. It was fifteen minutes later, minutes that had lasted the usual time but during which time meant very little. I can only say I had no idea what this was, or whether it was an illusion, a fantasy, or some trick of the mind. I went to the bathroom and took my temperature. It was normal. But in fact, although my mind doubted what I had heard, something deeper than my mind didn't. At that level, I knew whatever it was had not been a hallucination. I knew that it was real, even if it was incomprehensible. And so I put it away somewhere in my mind, somewhere that it could be remembered, if not understood.

And then, a few weeks later, I was at Mass, in the church I usually go to, kneeling after Communion, and drifting aimlessly in my thoughts. As I often do, I looked haphazardly toward the altar, and at the marble behind the sacristy, at the white cross set in the emerald circle. And then, suddenly, there it was again, unmistakably the same thing, only this time far more fleeting and less intense—the same sudden fixation on a space, the same intensity of color, not a different color, but the same color somehow more concentrated, as if the atoms were suddenly imploding on one area, creating something completely different yet completely the same, as if reality did not cede to something else in that space but became more itself, more fully itself, more connected with itself. And then the tone again, the tone of voice, the insistence that I hear it, the sense of calm and urgency, the sense of warning and intimacy, the sense of judgment, and unimaginable concern. And then again, it went, and the space and the color became less itself, and the music became less itself, and the Communion became less itself. And I did not understand any of it.

Two weeks later, I walked into my doctor's office and my life changed for good. The news of my HIV infection was the last thing I expected, and the first thing I feared. It instantly altered my vision. It was like being in a movie theater when something goes wrong in the projector room, and suddenly the film slips, and the images are out of focus and slipping haphazardly beneath the screen, and the light flickers and the figures jump. And you wait for it to be fixed, for the movie to jump back into its space, for the story to go back to itself, for the scenes that have already been lost to be pieced together in retrospect. And you wait and wait. And then it dawns on you that, in fact, the movie will never be fixed, that from now on, this *is* the movie, and that from now on, you will have to find a way to watch it differently, to adjust your eyes and vision and hearing, to glean from its new disorder an order that you can remember and comprehend.

Or it was like a cartoon, where the horizon shifts unpredictably back and forth, so that you can never quite know where you stand in relationship to anything else, how close they are or how far. Only it is worse than that because you cannot simply watch this cartoon; you have to walk into it, you have to put one foot in front of the other, not knowing where or what true space is, or if the place you are about to enter is actually where you think it is, or whether in the time it takes for you to put one foot forward, the ground will actually slip away from or toward you. And so I found myself in the days and weeks after the news literally looking at the ground as I walked, trying to find a security in a physical reliability, now that the mental one had escaped me.

In this sudden new world, it was difficult to know any-thing. I tried to sleep but the awareness of the news woke me up, rising like a tide of anxiety through my sleep until it jolted me into panicked consciousness. They tell you that it is at moments like this that faith matters, and people who do not have faith even believe that it is for the sake of such moments that you have faith to begin with. What is the use of faith, after all, if it cannot be a support when the world collapses from under you? But for me, at least, faith has never been like that. At the moments I have needed it most, it has slipped quickly away from me, it has receded into a terrible loneliness and fear. And so it was at this time. It wasn't that I lost faith; it wasn't that it forced me to some sudden epiphany; it was just that it wasn't there, or I didn't think it was there. The bleakness that leads to faith somehow replaces faith in the moments you need most to escape it.

And so my friends came to help me. They gave me a bed and an ear; they even wandered into my life aimlessly and wandered out again; they lay down on the grass with me and looked vacantly at the sky; they heard me sob, and saw me physically convulse in shock. And one in par-ticular came over one morning, someone who had once been close to me but who had drifted somewhat apart, and I told him the news. And it took a few seconds for it to sink in, but as it did, his face collapsed and he said, quite simply, and quite clearly, "Andrew, Andrew," and in the timbre of his words, and in the repetition of the name and in the mixture of concern and disappointment, shock and warmth, I recognized at once the voice, instantly and shockingly, and I recognized the tone. And then a few days later still, this time on the phone, another person in my life responded to the news in exactly the same way—"Andrew, Andrew"—a lament, an invitation, a sudden acknowledgment of what had until then been undetectable. And I heard it again; and I knew where it was from.

And then a few days later, when for the first time I actually sat down and prayed, I found myself with a copy of the Bible, and like some schoolboy, flipping through it for some sort of comfort, I came haphazardly upon the end of Luke's Chapter 10. And this is what I found myself reading:

> In the course of their journey he came to a village, and a woman named Martha welcomed him into her house. She had a sister called Mary, who sat down at the Lord's feet and listened to him speaking. Now Martha who was distracted with all the serving said, "Lord, do you not care that my sister is leaving me to do the serving all by myself? Please tell her to help me." But the Lord answered, "Martha, Martha," he said, "you worry and fret about so many things, and yet few are needed, indeed only one. It is Mary who has chosen the better part; it is not to be taken away from her."

"Martha, Martha." I don't think Jesus ever speaks to anyone else in the Gospels that way. "Martha, Martha." He repeats the name twice, exasperated but loving, admonitory but intimate. It's one of those many details that convince me that so much of the Gospels is true, the kind of intimate, intensely personal way of speaking, a detail that would never have been invented by someone trying to bludgeon the reader into some didactic lesson, the kind of address that a real person once used for a real person, and a real person he loved, as much as for her faults as in spite of them. "Martha, Martha." "Andrew, Andrew." It is not the tone simply of love; it is the tone of friendship, an unmistakable tone, a tone that I did not only recognize but suddenly, heartbreakingly, knew.

IN CAMUS'S NOVEL *The Plague,* his description of how plagues end is particularly masterful. We expect a catharsis, but we find merely a transition; we long for euphoria, but we discover only relief, tinged with, in some cases, regret and depression. For some, there is a zeal that comes with the awareness of unsought-for liberation, and the need to turn such arbitrary escape into meaningful creation. For many more, there is even—with good reason— a resistance to the good news itself because "the terrible months they had lived through had taught them prudence." The reactions to the news, Camus notes, are "diverse to the point of incoherence." Many refuse to believe that there is any hope at all, burned by dashed expectations one time too many: "[They were] imbued with a skepticism so thorough that it was now a second nature; they had become allergic to hope in any form. Thus even when the plague had run its course, they went on living by its standards. They were, in short, behind the times." Others found the possibility of an end too nerve-racking to bear and almost dared the plague to kill them before it was too late: "the rising wind of hope, after all these months of durance and depression, had fanned impatience to a blaze and swept away their self-control . . . and in the frenzy of their haste they tried to outstrip the plague, incapable of keeping pace with it up to the end."

And of course, we felt many of the same things, and with much the same incoherence. When I first wrote that it was possible to conceive of the end of the plague, the response among many gay men was so publicly hostile it took my breath away. But privately, it was all anyone spoke of. AIDS activists who, in the press, berated anyone who ventured optimism confidentially asked each other what they were going to do with their lives, now that the emergency had passed. As Camus noticed, "one of the signs that a return to the golden age of health was secretly awaited was that our fellow citizens, careful though they were not to voice their hope, now began to talk—in, it is true, a carefully detached tone—of the new way of life that would set in after the plague."

But this end, of course, was laden with paradox. As the plague relented in one world, it was busy redoubling its might in another, in countries far away, and against people who had nothing with which to counter it. In some ways, the moral predicament became more acute, as treatments existed but were too expensive to convey to the new millions suddenly in need. And each day, fresh victims were added to the list, people initiated into a disease that was suddenly, shockingly, less dramatic; people who would never suffer quite the paroxysm of fear of a decade earlier, but were also denied the solidarity such fear provided; people who complained that, unlike the veterans of the 1980s, they were not "on the team"; people who got infected who "should have known better"; people for whom the new treatments suddenly did not work or seemed to fail within months.

I think of a friend who was a Catholic priest in the Midwest, adored by his parishioners, a tireless organizer and often inspired homilist who, like so many of his fellow priests, was also homosexual. Very few of his parishioners knew this, and even fewer of his superiors. But in his early thirties, he was almost a model of the new Church, reaching out to the poor, restoring beauty to the liturgy, a favored son in a large Catholic family, and so officially beyond reproach. But he was also a serious person, and as he grew older, the contradictions of his calling intensified. His superiors could not see what the conflict was; since celibacy was demanded of all priests, straight and gay, they failed to grasp why my friend found his responsibilities any more difficult than his heterosexual colleagues. And when he went to his elders for advice and support, they merely offered him incomprehension and praise.

But of course, the issue was not celibacy. The issue was integrity: how a man dedicated to the Gospels could represent an institution that preached something he knew to be false about the dignity and equality of a section of humanity—and especially when he was a part of that section. And so, after a growing spiritual crisis, he sought a leave of absence from his parish, a time to think and pray and reflect on the path he had chosen. But as this leave began, the loneliness intensified, and one day in 1996, he found himself cut off from friends and family, unable to

lean on parishioners who had no qualms in leaning on
him, and traveling to a nearby city to be with a handful of
gay friends who might provide some kind of relief from
the strain. But the friends weren't there; and as the day
stretched before him, he found himself going to a bath-
house, where in a desperate attempt to find a moment
of intimacy, he had sex with someone he hardly knew,
and without precautions he knew he had to take. Heaven
knows what pressure led him to such an act of reck-
lessness or what psychological burdens propelled him
toward it. But within days, he was in a hospital, racked by
the telltale signs of a seroconversion fever that attacked
him with a vehemence that did not let up for the better
part of a month.

Now, a year later, the miracle drugs aren't working. His
body, overwhelmed by virus, has never managed to find
its footing. Twice, he collapsed with anemia, as AZT
played havoc with his blood, and he was rushed to the
hospital for a transfusion. Although the treatments have
lowered the amount of virus in his body, they haven't
made it undetectable, and his body is buffeted with side
effects that effectively prevent him from leading a completely normal life. The fact that he got infected when the
plague was declared over did not make his plight psychologically less agonizing. Indeed, the sense of being, in
Camus's words, "behind the times," of being trapped between hope and failure, was merely a different form of
torment, and no less acute because the world he now in-
habited was breathing an enormous sigh of relief.

And even now, among my friends, there are those who
refuse to be tested for a virus that can be almost wiped

out from the bloodstream; and there are those whose bodies reveal low but still detectable levels of virus, and who are unsure of when and how and if it will return with a vengeance; and those who, with undetectable levels of the virus, have clicked their minds into believing that they are no longer even infected, and expose their sexual partners to a viral strain made more lethal by its resistance to the new generation of drugs. And there are those who, sensing an abatement of the pressure, have returned, almost manically, to unsafe sexual behavior, as if terrified by the notion that they might actually survive, that the plague might end, and, with it, the solidarity that made it endurable. And those still who, fearful of losing disability insurance, have actually stopped effective treatment so that they will remain at permanent risk of death, preferring to cling to the familiarity of illness than face the difficult and mundane challenges of building a new life.

And as these reactions proliferated, the bonds of connection have begun ineluctably to fray. A friend in New York, positive for ten years, contemplates breaking up with his boyfriend because he suddenly realizes he is going to live. "I felt safe where I was," he told me. "But now I feel like an attractive person again. It's more what you're radiating inside—the feeling that, finally, you're not a potential burden. I mean, maybe I'm not a potential burden." The divisions between positive and negative men still endure; even among the positive, there are those who are detectable and those who are not, those whose T cells are recovering and those whose T cells are not. Relationships break up; courtships dissipate; as people begin to contemplate a new life free of grief, the triage of personal separation continues, made more cruel by the optimism that makes it possible. Another friend, this one an AIDS activist of hardened credentials, confessed that he felt the meaning of his life slipping away from him. "At some point, you just have to go on," he said, with little irony. "You say that was a great period in your life, but it's a big world, and at some point you have to find a way to slip back into it and try and be a happy citizen . . . What I want is a boyfriend I love, a job that doesn't make me crazy, and good friends."

I remember visiting San Francisco this past Halloween. I was curious to see how it would feel to be there, at a time when the epidemic hung in animated suspension above the streets it once devastated. And what more appropriate time, I thought, than the day of the dead, the night when the boundaries between the dead and the living are supposed to slip, merge, and blur into something more subversive than normality?

And yet it seemed so normal. The crowds in the Castro, if anything, seemed lackluster, and strained. The obligatory drag queens and mock-Christs, with their routine attempt at irrelevant blasphemy, the belly-bulging muscle bears and silver-sprayed grim reapers were swamped by a mass of stumbling, stoned straight kids, blearily crashing into each other in the streets. To the casual observer, it looked like a somewhat uninspired but still lively street festival. But to me (and maybe this was a projection), there was also an air of wistfulness about the place, a barely repressed exhaustion, a going through of the motions.

Surely grief had something to do with it. Even the room

I was crashing in was filled with the bric-a-brac of a friend's dead lover, left almost exactly as my friend remembered it, as if to win him back, his paintings on the walls, his obituary framed carefully on the bookshelf. This man had been in a new relationship for the better part of three years, but his old one had not yet ended, and it had certainly not evaporated upon death. And every friend I saw in the few days I was there carried someone with him, some echo that refused to die away, or a virus that carried in its very genes the imprint of yet another corpse, the pathogen of yet another spasm of need, met somewhere. This grief, like the virus, was undetectable, as we learnt to say. But just because it was undetectable didn't mean it wasn't there.

Camus saw this too. The protagonist of his visionary novel, Dr. Rieux, confronted the end of the plague by witnessing the death of his friend, Tarrou. Just when he should have been declaring victory, the doctor was presented with an undeniable defeat. Rieux sensed in the air, as one could sense over the streets of San Francisco, a silence that obliterated the relief, a silence of people gone and never to return, a silence that makes victory over such an atrocity an almost meaningless event: "There as here, it was the same solemn pause, the lull that follows battle; it was the silence of defeat. But the silence now enveloping his dead friend, so dense, so much akin to the nocturnal silence of the streets and of the town set free at last, made Rieux cruelly aware that this defeat was final, the last disastrous battle that ends a war and makes peace itself an ill beyond all remedy."

*

I WOULD LIKE TO WRITE about all this without writing about sex, but it would not be honest. In one important sense, AIDS was, for the better part of a decade, a plague. It affected large numbers of people, who could do little or nothing about it, and it slowly killed them. For a while, it had a subcultural democracy about it. You couldn't buy your way out of it or easily avoid it. And the treatments were, to a greater or lesser extent, useless. But in another sense, it wasn't, strictly speaking, a plague. Unlike the Spanish flu or the Black Death, it was not entirely random because it was spread by sex, and sex has rarely been understood to be as neutral an activity as shaking hands or breathing the air. Nor, of course, should it. The meeting of two human beings in a sexual encounter can never be a neutral or a casual phenomenon. It has meaning, and danger, and promise. It betokens a particular form of responsibility, as well as liberation. And when it also involves the risk of death, that responsibility—and that meaning—is even more profound.

We have been taught, of course, that this is a specious distinction, that privileging sex in this way is ineradicably "puritan," that it imputes false "innocence" to certain kinds of victims and a false guilt to others, and that plagues "do not discriminate." But, of course, this one did discriminate. Even now, when the spokesmen of the AIDS industry are tirelessly preaching the universality of AIDS in America, HIV infection remains remarkably confined to those groups of people it has always affected: homosexual men, intravenous drug users, and their sexual partners. Even now, in a world transformed by medical technology and precise information, a vast number of HIV infections in America still occur between one man and another in a sexual act.

And even now, when it is perfectly clear how one contracts HIV, and has been clear for the better part of a decade, a hefty proportion of the urban gay population remains infected, and the proportion shows no sign of sharply diminishing. I don't say this out of a desire to judge, although I know that is how, sadly, a great many people will hear it. But I think that if we deny that this persistence of disease is even troubling, we come close to saying that gay men seem incapable of saving themselves.

Yes, of course, the gay population dramatically changed its behavior in the early years of the epidemic; and even now the strictures of safer sex remain largely in place, and what has been called the "condom code" prevails. Gay men are not suicidal. But they are certainly not prepared to abolish all risk. The condom code is about as effective in combating infection as it is in combating unwanted pregnancy, and yet it remains the primary firewall against mass death. In fact, as the epidemic has "matured," we seem to have come to a kind of equilibrium in which a steady, if small, number of gay men continue to be infected and in which, because many HIV-positive men are living longer and longer, the proportion of all homosexuals infected with HIV grows larger still. Just as an acceptable level of violence becomes ingrained in societies beset with terrorism, so an acceptable level of disease seems to have become ingrained among gay men. And that can hardly fail to worry, if not terrify.

This applies, of course, as much to me as anyone else. I contracted the disease in full knowledge of how it is transmitted, and without any illusions about how debilitating and terrifying a diagnosis it could be. I had witnessed first-hand a man dying of AIDS; I had seen the ravages of its impact and the harrowing humiliation it meant. I had written about it, volunteered to combat it, and tried to understand it. But I still risked getting it. And the memories of that risk and the ramifications of it for myself, my family, and my friends still force me into questions I would rather not confront, and have expended a great deal of effort avoiding. This is, of course, an understandable reaction, if not a defensible one. I remember in particular the emotional spasm I felt at the blithe comment of an old and good high school friend of mine, when I told him I was infected. He asked who had infected me; and I told him that, without remembering any particular incident of unsafe sex, I didn't really know. The time between my negative test and my positive test was over a year, I explained. It could have been anyone. "*Anyone*?" he asked incredulously. "How many people did you sleep with, for God's sake?"

Too many, God knows. Too many for meaning and dignity to be given to every one; too many for love to be present at each; too many for sex to be very often more than a temporary but powerful release from debilitating fear and loneliness. My heterosexual friend, of course, instinctively saw my sexual life as a concession to carnality, an unthinkable lapse into irresponsibility—and I do not wish to deny that at some obvious level, it was. And

I don't want to disclaim responsibility for it. But at a deeper level, it was also something more complicated than that, something that is as hard to understand dispassionately as it is to experientially escape. But understanding promiscuity is a necessary first step to transforming it, and transforming it into something more meaningful and dignified and loving is, perhaps, the most difficult bequest of the last two decades.

But let me say at first that the easy outs, I fear, are too easy, on either side. Some might say, for example, that my active sexual life was a simple response to guilt and self-hatred, that my escapades were a form of adolescent revolt against a moral and religious teaching which I tried hard to live up to but failed to fulfill. But this is wrong in one simple respect. With regard to homosexuality, I inherited no moral and religious teaching that could guide me to success or failure. In my adolescence and young adulthood, the teaching of the Church was merely a silence, an increasingly hollow denial even of the existence of homosexuals, let alone a credible ethical guide to how they should lead their lives. It is still true that in over thirty years of weekly churchgoing, I have never heard a homily that attempted to explain how a gay man should live, or how his sexuality should be expressed. I have heard nothing but a vast and endless and embarrassed silence, an awkward, unexpressed desire for the simple nonexistence of such people, for their absence from the moral and physical universe, for a word or a phrase, like "objective disorder," that could simply abolish the problem they represented and the diverse humanity they symbolized. The teaching I inherited was a teaching that, in the best of all possible worlds, I simply would not exist. And it was hard to disobey this; since it was not an order, it was merely a wish.

If articulated, I suppose, the order was abstinence. Abstinence forever; abstinence always; abstinence not for the sake of something else, but for its own sake; abstinence not just from sex, but from love and love's hope and the touch of a lover's embrace. Abstinence even from recognition, acknowledgment, family. Some were honest enough to describe this fate as emblematic of Jesus' suffering on the cross, and they invited you to participate in it and told you to embrace it. And they did so with a sympathy that was no less cruel for being genuine. But Jesus' suffering was at least *for* something, for forgiveness, for universal redemption, remaining in his desperate isolation on the cross a symbol of human brokenness who opened his pinioned arms to everyone. It was an act of eternal solidarity with the suffering, not an arbitrary invitation to the ordeal, let alone a glorification of it.

And this condescension was intensified by the uniqueness of its message. No other group was called to celibacy for the sake of nothing. Priests and religious were asked to abandon physical love in order to make themselves more fully able to receive God's love and to give it back to their flock. They were not asked, like homosexuals, to deny themselves human intimacy merely for the sake of self-sacrifice. And no other group of people was told that although they did not choose their condition, it precluded them from the most sacred and sustaining relationships known to man. The infertile were prayed for, and married, and embraced; the sick and wounded were celebrated and invoked as models; the pariahs were welcomed into the fold; the prodigal sons were counted more joyously than the regular parishioners. But the homosexuals were unmentioned and unmentionable. For them, the exclusion from the healing power of love was matched only by an exclusion from official, articulated sympathy.

There were moments when this exclusion did more than condescend; it suffocated. I remember in particular a moment at Mass only a few years ago, when the AIDS quilt came to Washington. I had spent the afternoon on the Mall, remembering friends, reading names, fearing the worst. And I went from the quilt to Mass, where by some spectacular coincidence, the reading was about Jesus' healing of lepers. Of ten lepers Jesus healed, only one thanked him, a Samaritan, a man doubly stigmatized, not simply by his illness but by his social marginalization. And the sermon, in a parish in the heart of Washington's gay neighborhood, in the middle of a plague that had decimated hundreds of parishioners, began with these words: "Today, few of us know the meaning of a plague like leprosy. Thanks to modern science, it has largely been cured. And in our society, leprosy fails to attract any further stigma and nothing approximates it. So in order to understand the meaning of a story like this, we have to think of modern afflictions like cancer or lung disease." At the end of the Mass, I walked up to the priest, shaking with anger. "Have you heard of AIDS, Father?" I asked. "It's in the papers." "Well," he said. "I didn't think it would affect anyone here."

I mention this merely to insist upon the silence—not necessarily hostility, or hatred, or bigotry—merely silence. Sometimes you have listen to silence to hear it.

Sometimes a doctrine that is rarely expressed or explained or even articulated, a doctrine that is even proclaimed by people whose own lives are testaments to a different sexual orientation, a doctrine that seeks to extinguish love from the hearts of a whole segment of humanity, is so onerous and invidious and anomalous that silence is its only decent expression. But it is and was this silence that defined for me, and still defines for millions, the ethic for a homosexual life in America and around the world. Which is to say, it is an unethic, a statement that some people are effectively beneath even the project of an ethical teaching.

This is the necessary context in which any discussion of homosexual sex has to take place, in a plague, before a plague, or after a plague. And the context is, for most gay children and adolescents, in most respects, a vacuum. In this vacuum, extremes find a natural home, extremes of despair and extremes of abandon. Of course, in my case, the vacuum was a Catholic one. But in some respects, the Protestant vacuum was even more airless. For those for whom Leviticus was not merely a document for interpretation but a literal manual for life, the options were less exquisitely balanced than in the Catholic Church but more compellingly clear. With some fundamentalists, indeed, silence would have been an achievement. Their abstract demand that homosexuals be saved, their loving invitation to "leave" a "deception," could only serve to obliterate the integrity and self-respect of any gay child who heard them. The ministers who used such language certainly could not provide an ethic for homosexual living. They offered a way out, not a way forward. But what if the way out was unavailable? What options remained? What incentives were offered for you to choose one way of life over another, when all possible expressions of your identity, from love and fidelity to promiscuity and prostitution, were regarded as morally indistinguishable one from the other? How can a human being navigate an ethical life in the midst of such moral nihilism? The answer is an obvious one, made explicable only by the thought that, in the minds of such theologians, homosexuals aren't fully human beings at all.

I think of a friend of mine, a young, passionate, sweet-tempered man, who resolved his own sexual temptations by joining a Christian cult in college. As his sexuality emerged in his late teens, he found himself unable to meet other young men in a social context, and so he began to frequent public restrooms to find relief. The feelings he felt there were intensified not only by guilt but by need, the fleeting moments of contact a rare hint of a shared intimacy, and a shared hope. But that hope was immediately undermined by the simple knowledge that he was also ashamed and that the men around him were also ashamed. If they were not ashamed, after all, why were they there? Why were they hiding in stalls and bathrooms, defining themselves and their sexuality by a forbidden lust in a place designed for excrement? But despite the shame, he kept going back again and again, driven by needs he couldn't begin to control, alternately exhilarated and ashamed, entranced and appalled. Nothing else in his life promised such sweet relief or momentary bliss, but nothing else similarly forced him to split his life in two, to humiliate himself in the process of becoming a man. Until, that is, the shame finally overwhelmed the hope, and the contradictions of his life began to destroy its equilibrium and he found himself more and more desperately seeking an out.

And so he converted to fundamentalist Christianity, living with members of the cult, using its rituals to purge himself of the society and contact he craved, replacing the intimacy of sex with the intimacy of fanaticism. The only trouble was that the erotic feelings never declined, and the needs for a deeper contact never diminished. Not that he didn't try. At one point, he stopped masturbating for six months in a determined attempt to rid himself of his feelings. But then erotic dreams about men soaked his bed, dreams he could no more control than he could defy gravity. And so he gave himself an ultimatum and prayed that God would take these thoughts from him, and believed that if they didn't disappear, he would take it as a sign that God had clearly condemned him. And so it was, after another month of failure, that he came to leave the campus one day, with a mound of sleeping pills, and collapse in a distant field, until, by complete chance, he was found and rushed to hospital. His was an ineluctably Protestant fate. The kind of ethical vacuum to which his religion had abandoned him left him little choice but to stop living altogether. He could not be saved; so he chose to be damned. He was not alone. He is not alone.

Of course, in adulthood, we found out something more complicated about the teachings of the Church. We were introduced to the formula now recited as the immediate defense to charges of cruelty or exclusion: "hate the sin, love the sinner." In the 1970s and '80s the churches began to articulate a more nuanced approach to homosexuality, and by the 1990s this process reached its apogee. The teaching, in a nutshell, was that homosexual persons deserved respect and love and honor, but that what they "did" could never be countenanced. For fundamentalist Protestants, the formula was to embrace the sinner and passionately attempt to rescue him from what was called the "lifestyle," which was defined as one of promiscuous sodomy. And so the ethical silence was eventually broken; the vacuum filled with a whisper of air.

But a question lingered: Was there oxygen in that air? And what could it possibly *mean* to love the sinner but hate the sin? In the first place, it had to mean that homosexuality was essentially about sex. If homosexuality was defined as an "innate" inclination to commit a sin, then that sin had to be defined as an act of genital contact with a person of the same sex. So, of course, this isolated and, to many, repulsive activity was easily separated from the human person who performed it. It was "sexual activity behind closed doors," in the words of the leader of the Christian Coalition. It was a temporary lapse from an otherwise dignified life, a discrete and separable activity that could be condemned without in any way diminishing the sacred worth of the person who performed it. In fact, its very strangeness and repugnance only intensified the sense that rescuing someone from its carnal allure was essential to respecting that person in the first place.

But what if homosexuality was, in fact, more profoundly about love than about sex? What if it contained, like heterosexuality, all the nobility and failure of the search for intimacy and the need for affection? And what if sex was merely one, albeit profound, way of expressing that intimacy? How was it then possible to separate homosexuality from the dignity of the person? How was it possible to love someone and yet deny him the capacity for love himself? And for Christians?

For some Protestants and old-style Catholics, the response was simple. Homosexuals were incapable of love; they were sick and compulsive; their "love" was, in fact, a form of neurosis and needed to be cured, not mollified. I cannot address this argument now (I tackle it more fully in the next chapter), but, in any case, it was not the official position of the Catholic Church. That Church could not have been clearer in rejecting such a demeaning characterization of the nature of homosexuality. In the 1980s, Rome had taught unequivocally the inherent dignity of homosexual persons, and the importance of respecting them in a way that did not reduce their identity to mere sex. The Church never denied that an important component to homosexual life, as to the heterosexual life, was the human capacity and need for love. And in the late 1990s, in a striking development, the American Catholic bishops had gone one step further, speaking, in moving and historic tones, of the need for the parents of homosexual children to accept and love their child "as a gift of God; and [to accept] the full truth of God's revelation about the dignity of the human person and the meaning of human sexuality." If homosexuals were gifts of God, then how exactly were they incapable of love? And why was their sexuality intrinsically separable from the capacity for intimacy?

The answer could not be related to homosexuals' involuntary inability to procreate, because nonprocreative sex had already been sanctioned, indeed celebrated, for the infertile. So what could it be about? The truth was: nothing coherent. When you begin to see homosexuality not as some bizarre and willful attempt to practice a specific sexual act, but as a deep and complex part of a human person, a person who needs as much love and as much divine love as any other person, then it becomes clear how it is, in fact, impossible to hate the "sin" and love the "sinner." Or how the very formulation is, in fact, a way of denigrating homosexual people, denying their humanity, erasing their integrity. It is as if we were to say that we loved Jews, so long as they never went to a synagogue; or that we welcomed immigrants, so long as they never tried to learn English. It is a rejection masquerading as an acceptance, and it perpetuates, in the guise of alleviating, the very ethical conflict from which homosexuals are doggedly trying to escape.

So the sexual pathologies which plague homosexuals are not relieved by this formula; they are merely made more poignant, and intense. And it is no mystery why they are. If you teach people that something as deep inside them as their very personality is either a source of unimaginable shame or unmentionable sin, and if you tell them that their only ethical direction is either the suppression of that self in a life of suffering or a life of meaningless promiscuity followed by eternal damnation, then it is perhaps not surprising that their moral and sexual behavior becomes wildly dichotic; that it veers from compulsive activity to shame and withdrawal; or that it becomes anesthetized by drugs or alcohol or fatally distorted by the false, crude ideology of easy prophets. A friend remembers a moment long ago on the piers in New York City as he watched a young man submit to anonymous anal sex, at night, in the open air, in front of the water. And afterwards, as his invisible and wordless partner moved away into the darkness, the young man bent over and started sobbing. He was sobbing not just because he thought he had just done the most evil thing he could possibly do, but also because it was the thing he had most wanted to do ever since he became a self-conscious being. And he was spiritually and physically jackknifed by the experience, severed into two incompatible parts, presented with a chance of being himself but only at the expense of excising himself. No discussion of homosexual promiscuity makes sense without this context of contradictory needs, just as no discussion of heterosexual promiscuity makes sense without the context of marriage, love, and family.

And to flatten the meaning of this experience at the expense of the person's sense of morality or the person's need for love is not a solution to the problem. It's an abolition of the problem. The only tolerable human solution is to find a way that somehow connects the two, a way that allows a person to retain his sense of morality alongside his need for love. The trouble, of course, is that the homosexual's defenders have been as blind to this as his attackers. For at least two generations, the defenders of gay sexuality have been as indiscriminate in their defense as its opponents have been in their attack. One side has excoriated promiscuity; the other side has glorified it. And both have in the process erased the human being in the middle, erased his real dilemma, erased his real responsibility, erased the pull of his yearning and the reality of his self-control. How easy, after all, to posture over that man on the pier, to see in him either a self-hating homosexual or a self-destructive sinner—rather than as a complex moral and physical being, with needs and wants and the means, if not always the will, to direct them. Both puritan and anti-puritan judgments perform the function of reassuring the judges that their worldview is secure, their pedestal intact. But neither tells the truth about that man, which is that he is somewhere in between these ideologies, desperately seeking a way forward rather than a simple way out.

The gay liberationists have plenty to answer for in this. For far too long, they promoted the tragic lie that no avenue of sexuality was any better or nobler than any other; that all demands for responsibility or fidelity or commitment or even healthier psychological integration were mere covers for "neoconservatism" or, worse, "self-hatred"; that even in the teeth of a viral catastrophe, saving lives was less important than saving a culture of "promiscuity as a collective way of life," when, of course, it was little more than a collective way of death. They demeaned gay men almost as surely as their unwitting allies, the fundamentalists. And they constructed and defended and glorified the abattoirs of the epidemic, even when they knew exactly what was going on. Yes, of course, because their ultimate sympathy lay with those trapped in this cycle, they were more morally defensible than condemning or oblivious outsiders. But they didn't help matters by a knee-jerk defense of catastrophic self-destruction, dressed up as cutting-edge theory. If the outside world was guilty of being an accomplice to AIDS by virtue of its negligence, then this inside world was guilty of being an accomplice by virtue of its knowledge. These insiders not only rationalized away a communal bloodbath; they justified the means for its continuance.

Perhaps this too was a response to guilt. There is little doubt that the ideology that human beings are mere social constructions and that sex is beyond good and evil facilitated a world in which gay men literally killed each other by the thousands. And there's little doubt that, for at least one generation, many gay men responded to the vacuum into which their families and their churches and their communities had thrown them, by internalizing this other vacuum of meaning and seeing in it an identity that could rescue them. Once this mechanism had started, once this trigger had been pulled, once every gay man had been absolved from responsibility for giving HIV to another gay man, then it was very hard to go back and admit a mistake. Because the crimes of this regime were so enormous, and their consequences so grave, it became unimaginable to address, let alone confront, the moral responsibility they entailed.

I do not want to excuse myself from this as well. Although I never publicly defended promiscuity, I never publicly attacked it. I attempted to avoid the subject, in part because I felt, and often still feel, unable to live up to the ideals I really hold. I argued instead for the ennobling and critical institution of marriage, without which I felt any argument against promiscuity would simply collapse against the mountain of social and psychological incentives against it. In this, I suppose, I am not atypical of many gay men. During the plague, we tried to exercise responsibility. Most of us, once the risks of transmission were known, never wittingly subjected another man to intolerable risk. After my infection, as before, I followed the condom code to the letter, did my best to be public about my HIV status and to tell most, if not all, of my sexual partners. If asked, I never lied. But it was amazing, perhaps, how infrequently I was asked.

In other words, I wore a bulletproof vest but continued to wander into the firing zone. And I refuse to see this in retrospect as a function either of triumphant queer rebellion or of pathological self-destruction. It was a position rooted in plague but also rooted in experiences far older and far deeper than plague. For twenty-three years of my life, sex was something bound up in my mind with an identity I couldn't claim and a release I didn't deserve. It was glimpsed through curtains, or in glances; it was intimated in friendship and hurt; it was defined by a notion of unavailability. I remember in high school seeing a friend's early beard turn into residual dark stubble and wondering, like a small child wonders about airplanes, how it would feel to be there. And so when it first came to be there, to be literally under the touch of my hands, it was inevitable perhaps that I should associate it with a bliss and an undoing that seemed to erase all that had gone before. And even now, ten years after that first undoing, I still find myself marveling at the exotic beauty of other men, at the literally unbelievable sense of having them, finding myself liberated once again by the memory of this puerile joy.

So my refusal to give this up, to return to what I had been, even in the face of undeniable terror and considerable risk, was not simply an act of intransigence or irresponsibility or even some unconscious attempt to punish myself. It was an act, at some level, of integrity. It was simply not possible for me to change my entire makeup, my history, my emotional needs, and my psychological development overnight—even under the threat of extreme danger. Or perhaps it would be better to say that it was not possible to do so without jettisoning a large part of myself, that part of myself that had finally allowed me to experience joy, and hope, and the promise of love.

Was sex too central a part of this self? Maybe. All I can say in defense is that those who have never known what it feels like to have their sexual identity smudged out from birth on, to have their innermost hopes reduced for years to the language of depravity, to have their yearnings for love defined as they grow up as unspeakable vice, the need for sexual intimacy and relief in adulthood may seem far less pressing. But for many homosexuals, these wounds are still fresh, and the salve is still needed. Which is why many gay men approach sex with a reverence and passion their heterosexual counterparts often misplace somewhere in their adulthood. And why even plague could not take it away.

So is this too complicated a thought? That although an activity cannot be fully justified in the abstract, it can be completely understandable, even necessary, in an actual life? And that a human being can live precisely in that knowledge, and know what he wants to attain, but live with the consequences of his failure? What, after all, was the alternative? The alternative was either to abandon all sense of responsibility, and rationalize it away in the slogans of amoral ideology, or to collapse one's life into the arid emptiness of complete self-denial, which is to say, to end one's life altogether. Yes, I longed for a relationship that could resolve these conflicts, channel sex into love and commitment and responsibility, but, for whatever reasons, I didn't find it. Instead, I celebrated and articulated its possibility, and did everything I could to advance the day when such relationships could become the norm. But in the meantime, I struggled, and failed, and struggled again—a paradigm that is not unfamiliar to anyone trying to live an ethical life.

Which is not to say that I found all sex—even casual sex—to be a baleful or destructive experience. Far from it. Just because I believe that sex is at its most humane and meaningful and real when it is expressed in love and fidelity, it does not follow that I believe that all sex outside such a context is inherently wrong or pernicious. Again, the way our culture has set up the debate—between puritans and libertines, between indiscriminate supporters of promiscuity and prophets of sexual doom—does no justice to life as it is actually lived, and to the human beings trying to navigate through it. It is, of course, far easier to thrust gay men into one of two camps—assimilationists or radicals, prudes or philanderers—than it is to observe who they actually are. But the more interesting questions, indeed the only interesting questions, lie somewhere in between.

It may seem particularly strange in our culture for people of faith to hold such a nuanced sexual ethic, but that, I think, says far more about our culture's simplification of religious life than it does about religious life itself. For my own part, the conflict between sex and faith has never been as conflicted as might at first appear. Like many Catholics, although I have always felt the spiritual and sexual lives to be, at the deepest level, in conflict, I have never seen that conflict to be irreparable in my life as I have lived it. Sexual experience, from the beginning, seemed to me almost a sacrament of human existence, a truly transforming experience in the adventure of being human; an insight into both what love may possibly be and what death almost certainly is. In the modern bourgeois world, it may even be the only avenue for true self-risk that is still available. And to physically invade another person, and to be invaded, to merge with another body, to abandon the distance that makes our everyday lives a constant approximation of loneliness, these experiences have never ceased to awe me. Far from seeing them as a simple negation of spirituality, I instinctively found them to be windows into it. They were not the same as spiritual events, but in their eclipsing and humbling power, they intimated to me a parable of human powerlessness and frailty. And so, in their way, I think they turned me toward, rather than away from, what persisted as my faith.

Catholicism for me was, from the beginning, a sacramental religion. By this, I mean that it was not about abstraction but about reality, not about words but about actions, not about the unreachable but about the physicality of the divine. This was, for me, the core of the teaching about the Incarnation, the astonishing idea that God might actually assume human flesh and feel the wind against his face, and salt against his lips. Catholicism was a religion about smell and sight and touch, from the incense I ignited as an altar boy to the bread and wine of the Eucharist, when, even now, each week, I am actually enjoined to take into my mouth the *body* of the Son of God. My initiation into this mystery, in a small English town, was not so much into the word of the Church but into its flesh: the crisply starched vestments that I prepared for the priest in the sacristy, the grimy dark wood we gripped in the pews, the blossoms that filled the churches and classrooms in springtime, the feel of candle wax on my fingers and numbness in my knees. When sexuality burst in upon this boyhood scene, I was not so uninformed as to be guileless, but I was also primed to embrace it as yet another manifestation of a sensualized spirituality. It came easily to me. And not despite my Catholicism, but *because* of it.

And as I grew older, and sex became an actuality rather than an ideal, I found that it approximated a joy I never felt elsewhere. I came to revere sexuality not just because it was so long forbidden to me, but because I could not control or nurture it, or even fully own it. Unlike my intelligence or my conduct or even my faith, it could not be nurtured; it resisted taming or educating. It slipped away from the mind; it stopped me thinking; it undid, temporarily, what has been called the "ordeal of consciousness." To give this up, even under the threat of death, would have been to give up being fully human. I don't mean by this an unmitigated defense of Dionysian excess. Even in the wake of the extraordinary pull of sexuality in my twentysomething self, I never tempted fate, I practiced safer sex almost neurotically, as so many of my fellows did. I simply refused to take cover completely, to end any sexual adventurism, to abolish all risk. Like those inhabitants of Sarajevo who, after months of siege and the constant threat of snipers, began once again to walk down the streets slowly and upright and in full view, I rebelled against the logic of plague and judgment. There was foolishness in this, of course. But also an unrepentant assertion of freedom, an assertion that the deepest personal struggles do not end in the middle of a crisis. Indeed, in the middle of a crisis, a refusal to end them is a mark of the ultimate resistance.

And when the end seemed to arrive, resistance found another way. I remember one winter afternoon, not so long ago, when an old friend of mine and I spent the day together. We strolled the streets of Washington and talked of the life that seemed unexpectedly to stretch ahead of us. My friend had been positive for nearly a decade—since his college days. Together, we had lost the people closest to us and had at many points contemplated going the same way ourselves. But we were still here, both well and happy, both with "undetectable" virus and an unknowable future. Although we had always been drawn to one another, and long enjoyed each other's company the timing had never been right to embark on a relationship which went beyond the borders of friends and allies and supporters. But in this moment of transition, things began to change between us as well.

And as night fell, we found ourselves suddenly, unexpectedly in an embrace that lasted longer than it should have. The relief of survival, the knowledge of survival, was suddenly too much. We found ourselves holding each other almost as if we were all each of us had left, and with a need and a relish that took both of us by surprise. There was so much joy in it and so much sadness that it is difficult to express what it was that we actually felt, and since it could not be put into words, we did not put it into words. There are times when only bodies can express what minds cannot account for. So we kissed and embraced and clung to each other in silence. And as the passion grew, we found ourselves, without a word between us, taking the embrace still further and still further until, for the first time in each of our lives, as our bodies came together, we did not bother to reach for protection, and intimated in a single, mutual, liberating smile that not even the caution of so many years would bring anything any longer between us. "Are you sure?" he asked me. "Yes, I'm sure," I replied. No other words were necessary. And the barrier broke at last. And the fear was rebuked at last.

A DIFFERENCE BETWEEN the end of AIDS and the end of many other plagues: for the first time in history, a large proportion of the survivors will not simply be those who escaped infection, or were immune to the virus, but those who contracted the illness, contemplated their own death, and still survived. If for some this might lead to bitterness, for others it suggests something else entirely. It is not so much survivor guilt as survivor responsibility. It is the view of the world that comes from having confronted and defeated the most terrifying prospect imaginable and yet surviving. It is a view of the world that has seen the darkest possibilities for homosexual—and heterosexual—existence and now sees the opposite: the chance that such categories could be set aside, that the humanity of each could inform the humanity of the other.

Take Greg Scott, a Washingtonian I've known for years. As the plague unfolded, we both came of age, and it affected us in different ways. Greg was from a traditional Southern family, and when he was thrown out of the Marine Corps for homosexuality, he threw himself into years of furious activism. When I first came to know him, he was renowned in D.C. for hanging around bars, staring wildly at passersby, either as a prelude to lecturing or seducing them. For a short period of time, he would follow me around D.C. screaming, "Collaborator!" to punish me for the sin of writing or voicing politically incorrect views. But we both knew, at some level, that we were in the epidemic together, and so when I saw him slowly decline over the following years, I felt a part of myself decline as well. And as the days and months went by, I half expected to see Greg's face in the crowded obituary columns of the local gay paper, along with the dozens of other faces I had known or seen over the years. When I wrote an op-ed in 1995, hailing the latest breakthroughs in AIDS research, Greg had come up to me again in a bar and regaled me with the idiocy of my optimism. "This is not a survivable disease!" he yelled over the music. "What do you know about it anyway?" We had made an uneasy peace over the years, but his anger was still there, simmering below the surface of his crazed anxiety.

So I'd learnt to avoid Greg, as far as I could. I never relished our meetings. Since for a long time, he didn't know I was positive too, our conversations had this false air about them. The real solidarity I felt was one that I could not fully express—and it ate away at me. I occasionally spotted him, of course, walking his dog in the neighborhood, his body, always thin, now skeletal, his large, staring eyes disfigured by lesions, his gait that of a sixty-year-old. When my parents visited, I pointed him out from a distance on the street, in some doomed attempt to help them understand: "See. That's my friend Greg." Read: "See. That's my friend, Greg. Do you see what this is doing to us?" Eventually, Greg was taking morphine four times a day. He was on a regimen of sixty pills a day and virtually bedridden. So when I first caught sight of him in the spring of 1996, I literally jumped.

A few years before, as I've said, I'd become used to the shock of seeing someone I had known suddenly age twenty or thirty years in a few months. But all at once, the reverse was occurring. People I'd grown used to seeing hobbling along, their cheekbones poking out of their skin, their eyes deadened and looking down, were suddenly restored into some bizarre spectacle of health, gazing around as amazed as I was to see them alive. Or you'd see them in the gym, some skin infections still lingering, but their muscles slowly growing back, their skull-faces beginning to put on some newly acquired flesh. This is what Greg now looked like, his round, blue eyes almost tiny in his wide, pudgy face, his frame larger than I ever remembered it: bulky, lumbering, heavy. And the first time I bumped into him after his transformation, I could tell he was changed. The anger had somehow gone; a calm had replaced it. As we parted, we awkwardly hugged. This was a new kind of solidarity—not one of painful necessity, but of something far more elusive. Hope, perhaps? Or merely the shared memory of hopelessness?

From then on, I became used to Greg describing the contours of what he calls his "second life." The successive physical and material losses of his illness stripped him, he recalled, of everything he once had, and allowed him, in a way that's unique to the terminally ill, to rebuild himself from scratch. "There were times I was willing to accept that it was over," he told me. "But things were never fully tied up. There were too many things I had done wrong, things I wanted to amend, things I still wanted to do. I was hanging on tenaciously out of some moral judgment of myself, because I knew I hadn't got it right the first time."

In his progressive illness, Greg had lost first his energy, then his ability to digest food, then his job, then his best friend, and then most of his possessions, as he sold them off to pay for medications. But he hung on. "In the early days," he remembered, "I couldn't imagine going through all that shit to stay alive. My friend Dennis would say that

I'd never go that far. But then he died. Looking back, it's absurd the lengths I went to. I'd never realized I cared so much about myself." Greg's story brings to mind another friend, whose illness finally threatened his sight, and who had to decide, at one point, whether he wanted to pursue treatment. The treatment in question was a needle injection of a liquid directly into the eyeball. In other words, he had to watch as the needle came closer and closer and finally penetrated his eye. I remember asking him how on earth he could go through with it. "But I want to see," he told me, simply.

"When you're in bed all day, you're forced to consider what really matters to you." Greg elaborated: "When the most important thing you do in a day is your bowel movement, you learn to value every single source of energy . . . You go into yourself and you feel different from other people, permanently different." Some gains are subtle. "It sparked a new relationship with my grandmother. Like me, she was suddenly finding she couldn't drive her car anymore—so we bonded in a way we'd never bonded before. You suddenly see how people are valuable. I mean, if you're healthy, who has time for this old lady? And suddenly this old lady and I have so much in common. And I still have that. That's a gain. I have an appreciation and love for her that I never fully had before." Others were deeper. "My grandfather would say, 'You don't squeak under the bottom wire unless you're meant to.' And I feel that there's this enormous responsibility on me that I've never felt before . . . And it's a pleasant responsibility. I mean, lay it on me."

Responsibility was, perhaps, an unusual word to come

out of Greg's lips, and, until AIDS, it was not one usually associated with homosexuality. Before AIDS, gay life—rightly or wrongly—was identified with freedom from responsibility, rather than its opposite. Gay liberation was most commonly understood as liberation from the constraints of traditional norms, almost a dispensation that permitted homosexuals the absence of responsibility in return for an acquiescence in second-class citizenship. This was the Faustian bargain of the pre-AIDS closet: straights gave gays a certain amount of freedom; in return, gays gave away their self-respect. But with AIDS, responsibility became a central, involuntary feature of homosexual life. Without it, lovers would die alone, or without proper care. Without it, friends would contract a fatal disease because of lack of education. Without it, nothing would be done to stem the epidemic's wrath. In some ways, even the seemingly irresponsible outrages of ACT UP were the ultimate act of responsibility. They came from a conviction that someone had to lead, to connect the ghetto to the center of the country, because it was only by such a connection that the ghetto could be saved.

And in the experience of plague, what Greg felt on a personal level was repeated thousands of times. People who thought they didn't care for each other found that they could. Relationships that had had no social support were found to be as strong as any heterosexual marriage. Men who had long since gotten used to throwing their own lives away were confronted with the possibility that they actually did care about themselves and wanted to survive and failed to see themselves as somehow inferior to their heterosexual peers. A culture that had been based in some measure on desire became a culture rooted in strength. Of course, not everyone experienced such epiphanies. Some cracked; others died in bitterness or alone. Many failed to confront the families and workplaces and churches in ways that would have helped provide the capacity to survive. But many others did. And what didn't destroy them only made them less susceptible to condescension.

And as gay culture shifted in this way, so did gay politics. The radicalism of ACT UP segued into the radicalism of gays in the military and same-sex marriage. From chipping away at the edges of heterosexual acceptance, suddenly the central ramparts were breached. Once gay men had experienced beyond any doubt the fiber of real responsibility— the responsibility for life and death for themselves and others—more and more found it impossible to acquiesce in second-class lives. They demanded full recognition of their service to their country, and equal treatment under the law for the relationships they had cherished and sustained in the teeth of such terror. AIDS wasn't the only thing that created this transformation of gay demands, but it was surely linked to them at a profound psychological level.

Plagues and wars do this to peoples. They force them to ask more fundamental questions of who they are and what they want. Out of the First World War came women's equality. Out of the Second came the welfare state. Out of the Holocaust came the state of Israel. Out of cathartic necessity and loss and endurance comes, at least for a while, a desire to turn these things into something constructive, to appease the trauma by some tangible residue that can give meaning and dignity to what has happened.

Hovering behind the politics of homosexuality in the midst of AIDS and after AIDS is the question of what will actually be purchased from the horror. What exactly, after all, did a third of a million Americans die for? If not their fundamental equality, then what?

WHEN PEOPLE ASK ME why I became obsessed with the issue of marriage during the plague, I can only respond by saying that it had everything to do with this. Some have claimed that the strongest argument for marriage is that it would somehow "tame" homosexuals or "civilize" them, and, of course, in many ways, it is a classically conservative case for the institution. But it is revealing how very few conservatives have been able to make the argument, or have felt in any way comfortable with it. (You can count them on the fingers of one hand.) And those of us who have most persistently advocated it have been tagged with that allegedly oxymoronic term, "gay conservative," because it is easier to label than to listen. But, of course, equality in marriage, although it has conservative connotations, is not entirely a conservative project. It is not simply about "taming" or "civilizing" gay men. It is also the deepest means for the liberation of homosexuals, providing them with the only avenue for sexual and emotional development that can integrate them as equal human beings and remove from them the hideous historic option of choosing between their joy and their dignity. It is about deepening and widening and strengthening the possibility of true intimacy between two human beings.

And this, of course, is why many conservatives have intu-itively opposed it, as one might expect them to oppose all worrying moments of unpredictable liberation.

In plagues, as in wars, liberation is a particularly en-grossing idea. It comes to symbolize not only an end to the horror but a transcendence of it. As the years passed and the deaths mounted and my own immune system ticked vulnerably away, it was hard not to long for a liberation not just from part but from all of what the plague enforced. Perhaps, in other times, it would not have been necessary to grasp for such a complete liberation, or to feel its necessity so closely, or to try to figure out what exactly real liberation could mean. Before the plague, we had felt content to think of it as merely the temporary occasions of desire snatched in shadows, or the fleeting moments of cultural rebellion we had come to mistake for progress, or simply the quiet calm of an unexpected, pub-lic embrace. But as the plague grew, the depth of the expe-rience intimated a different depth of liberation. It was not enough any longer to experience love or to capture it. It was necessary to own it, and to have the love acknowl-edged.

Some have argued that this is an insistence too far, that homosexuals ask too much in demanding more than tol-eration. But acknowledgment, in love especially, is not a minor human need. Acknowledgment is enfranchisement, as every heterosexual spouse understands. So as the world was forced to acknowledge the reality of our deaths, we dared to dream it could acknowledge the reality of our lives.

I remember my first trip to see the AIDS quilt in 1987, when it was only a few thousand panels in size and fit comfortably in front of the White House. A handful of years later, as the epidemic crescendoed, it filled the entire Ellipse and beyond. In its final unveiling, in 1996, the tapestry spread from the Washington Monument to the steps of the Congress, arguably the largest work of memory ever assembled in America. And from the beginning to the end, the most dramatic change was not in the size of the memorial but in the crowds who visted it. In the first showing, the crowds were almost overwhelmingly homosexual. By the third, the presence of families—predominantly heterosexual—was overwhelming. The plague, which lasted longer than any presidency, was ignored by the first two presidents; the third one came quietly, acknowledging not simply the scale of the tragedy but its ability to humble and silence. And indeed, as you approached the quilt from the rest of the Mall, toward a place where tens of thousands of people congregated, noise actually subsided.

This extraordinary structure was not at the expense of gay culture, or of the quilt's gay identity, and, in this, it was a political metaphor for the hopes born of plague, as well as the despair it generated. It remained, from beginning to end, a subversive and buoyantly colorful piece of architecture. Unlike the Vietnam Memorial, which hovered nearby, it didn't immortalize its commemorated in regimental calligraphy. Its geography was not that remarkable black snowdrift of casualties, but a kind of chaotic living room, in which the unkempt litter of human beings—their jeans, photographs, glasses, sneakers, letters—was strewn on the ground, as if expecting the people to whom it belonged to return. I remember people walking over this landscape, looking like tourists, caught between grief and curiosity, saying little, peering intently down at the ground.

The panels themselves were tacky and vital, and therefore more chilling: we were invited to grieve over faded Streisand albums, college pennants, grubby bathrobes, Hallmark verses, and an endless battery of silk-screened 1970s kitsch. Unlike the formulas of official memorials, each panel managed to speak its own language in its own idiom: you had to stop at each one and rethink. Camus suggested that the most effective way to conceive of large numbers of deaths was to think of them in terms of movie theaters, but the quilt dispensed with such mind games by simply reproducing shards of the lives of the fallen, like overheard private conversations. Some panels were made by lovers, others by parents, friends, even children of the dead; and some were made by those whose names appeared on them. "Life's a Bitch and Then You Die," quipped one.

Even the names themselves rebelled against any attempt to regiment them. In the program for the second showing, some people were identified with full names, others with first names, others with nicknames. There were sixteen Keiths and one Uncle Keith, twenty-eight Eds, one Ed & Robert, eighty-two Davids, one David Who Loved The Minnesota Prairie, one mysterious David—Library of Congress, and one David—Happy Birthday. Some went only by two initials—T.J.; others spelled it out in full—Dr.

Robert P. Smith, Arthur James Stark Jr., HM1 James T. Carter USN; others were reduced to symbols—five stars (unnamed) "commemorating five theater people who died"; still others were summoned up by nothing but a baseball cap and an epitaph. Celebrities, of course, crept in—in one visit, I counted four Sylvesters and twenty-nine Ryan Whites—but they were scattered randomly among their peers. The most piercing: Roy Cohn's. A simple inscription: "Bully. Coward. Victim."

The integration of the plague was enhanced by the unending ritual of everyday names over the loudspeaker, as friends and relatives and strangers read out the death roll. "Patrick J. Grace, Dan Hartland, Ron Lopez, Edwina Murphy, Mark Jon Starr, Billy." Many of the two-minute recitations ended in "and my brother and best friend" or "my sweet little sister" or some such personal touch. From time to time, a mother's voice cracked over "my precious son and best friend," and the visitors to the quilt stiffened at once, their throat caught in another, numb moment of unexpected empathy. I remember bumping into an acquaintance. "What's going on?" I asked, lamely. "Oh, just looking for friends."

Just when you were ready to sink into moroseness, however, the panels turned on you. Drag-queen creations—taffeta, pumps, and pearls embroidered across silk—jostled next to the overalls of manual workers and the teddy bears of show-tune obsessives. There was plenty of bawdiness, even eroticism, and a particularly humanizing touch you don't find in cemeteries: a lot of the spelling was wrong. Many of the epitaphs had a lightly ironic edge to them, coming close to a kind of death camp: "The Fabulous Scott

Tobin" and "Dennis. We Didn't Get to Know Each Other Very Well, and Now We Never Will." My favorite panel ornament was a Lemon Pledge furniture-polish can. Others simply shocked you into reality: "Hopefully the family now understands," inscribed beneath a pair of someone's jeans; "For the friend who still cannot be named—and for all of us who live in a world where secrets must be kept." And another: "You still owe me two years, but I forgive you and will always love you. I never located your parents. Maybe someone will see this and tell them."

But if the quilt was a monument to how much hadn't changed; it was also a testament to how much had. It was a physical expression of an integration that spread beyond the quilt's four corners, an integration made more profound by the intensity of the emotions that accelerated it. "I have done nothing wrong," as one panel put it. "I am not worthless. I do mean something." "This is my beloved son," echoed another, "in whom I am well pleased." The parents who had once felt merely embarrassment had come to feel pride, and even solidarity.

And one is forced to ask what such solidarity could ever possibly mean if it did not include an acknowledgment of the love of a child for another human being. There is a reason why, for parents, the wedding day of their son or daughter is an epochal event in the life of their family, unequaled by any other. Because it is the day when their child becomes finally enfranchised as someone like her parents; when her equality breaks finally through her dependence. It is, as we have come to say, the "happiest day of her life." Almost no other day matches it—in terms of the social support it generates, the friends and family it brings together, the sheer overwhelming public "Yes!" to the most private of sentiments it represents. Along with our births and deaths, it is the most faithfully recorded and publicly recognized rite of passage we experience. And it is a statement by our society that certain values count for more than others—that love matters more than money; that family matters more than success; that, even though we care about someone's financial well-being, or career achievements, or fame, or education, we care more that she is happy, that she has found someone who can help her be happy, that love has found a way to make her life meaningful in a way few other things can.

It is the mark of ultimate human respect; and its automatic, unthinking, casual denial to gay men and women is the deepest psychological and political wound imaginable. Perhaps it is because the plague forced us to see that such people are finally worthy of respect that this remaining indignity increasingly stood out so starkly. I know that, for me, this was the beginning and the end of my conviction in the matter. If my friends could muster this much dignity in death, why should they be automatically denied it in life?

I remember my friend Trey, a handsome, frenzied, brilliant graduate from Harvard. When I first met him, in 1990, he was in his mid-twenties in a doctoral program at the University of Pennsylvania and he wasn't hard to fall in love with. As my crush turned into something more serious, I remember a trip a bunch of his friends and I made to New York, where an evening full of margaritas and furious political arguments finally wound up in a midtown Latino bar. As we sat next to each other, our knees hovering near touch, my infatuation degenerating into a pathetic obsession, he began a sentence with the words, "When I found out I was HIV-positive . . . ," and I could feel my stomach sink. It was like getting into an elevator and pressing the Up button, only to feel your body lurch suddenly downward. He went on, "I don't date HIV-negative guys anymore. They can be great people, but they just don't understand . . ."

I didn't give up my pursuit, for a while at least, but the truth is, since I was still HIV-negative, I didn't understand. And as my infant love turned into a somewhat bruising rejection, for the first time in my life I almost felt a twinge of envy for someone whose disease had brought him such clarity and purpose. In the years that followed, our clumsy affection turned into a prickly but committed friendship, punctuated by livid political fights and easy, intimate dinners. Until, that is, he found someone positive to fall in love with, and planned, in the methodical, intense way Trey planned everything, to get married.

I remember the wedding well. For the better part of a decade, AIDS had not changed Trey's physical appearance. But in the months before his marriage, a metamorphosis took place. His eyes suddenly sank into his head, his skin suddenly fell into his bones, he developed that awful skull look of the AIDS-malnourished, as he found it increasingly hard to absorb any food. He was, in reality, slowly starving to death, but that didn't stop him from exchanging vows, from getting his Texas family together, from corralling his friends and associates, to affirm that he had finally found love and that ultimately this was what really mattered. It was not a political statement. If anything, Trey's views about matrimony would have

likely been a staccato diatribe against bourgeois homoge-
nization. It was a human statement, made more poignant
and more profound by the closeness of mortality.

Oddly enough, his once-estranged family understood
this better than we did, and the toasts from his brother
and father came far more naturally than the awkward
fumblings of his gay friends and old flames. Like those
hastily conducted weddings in concentration camps, it
wasn't about marriage as such. It was not about prop-
erty and family and convention and cohabitation. It was
not even about the future. It was about the presentness
of human dignity. And when, several months later, we all
gathered again in the same suits and tight collars for his
memorial service, we understood this more deeply and
more instinctively than we ever would have cared to
before.

This particular quality of marriage is one we have long
recognized, which is why it has always been granted in
free societies with no conditions attached. Marriage is not
granted to people so long as they live up to its responsibilities; and it is not taken away from them if they don't.
The right to marry is understood as a given, almost
definitional of both human autonomy and political citizenship. In American constitutional law, it is accorded a
status deeper and more fundamental even than the right
to vote or the right to free speech; it is deemed to be
lodged not in the Bill of Rights but in the Declaration of
Independence itself. And such a hallowed niche for it
makes perfect sense. For who in America could believe
they had a right to the "pursuit of happiness" if that right
did not also include the right to marry the person they

loved? Indeed, it has been understood—and rightly understood—that the denial of this right to anyone for any
reason is a violation of liberty so profound that it negates
that person's citizenship altogether. Hence the severity of
the Supreme Court's ruling in *Loving v. Virginia* when it
declared quite simply that the right to marry—or not
marry—a person of one's choice "resides with the individual and cannot be infringed by the State." "The freedom to marry has long been recognized," Justice Warren
ruled, "as one of the vital personal rights essential to the
orderly pursuit of happiness by free men." Marriage, he
continued, was "one of the basic civil rights of man, fundamental to our very existence and survival."

One of the *basic* civil rights of man. This does not, as
some would say, beg the distinction between interracial
marriage and marriage between two people of the same
gender. Justice Warren's statements were not about interracial marriage; they were about marriage. Which is why
the furious debate that engulfed the twilight of the
plague was not about some nonexistent entity called "gay
marriage"; it was quite simply about marriage, and about
the right for everyone, heterosexual or homosexual, to
lay claim to the dignity and equality it uniquely represents. And *if* the love of one man for another and one
woman for another is as good and as meaningful and as
committed as that of one woman for one man, then there
is no conceivable reason why it should be granted to one
and denied the other.

But that "if" of course is the rub. At the root of all the
objections to equality in marriage is a simple and abiding
conviction—a conviction deep in the minds and hearts of

many homosexuals as well as heterosexuals—and that conviction is, quite baldly, that homosexual love is simply lesser than heterosexual love, and therefore cannot be accorded the same fundamental social recognition. Which is to say that, at the deepest, emotional level, homosexual persons are simply lesser than heterosexual persons; and that, at a political level, homosexual citizens are simply lesser than heterosexual citizens. Just as the ban on interracial marriage was not ultimately about marriage as such but about the simple notion of the inferiority—political and human—of blacks to whites, so the ban on same-sex marriage is not really about marriage as such either but about the simple inferiority of homosexuals to heterosexuals. It is that basic. The real question is not why we should be surprised by the assumptions behind the objection, but that it should have taken us so long to recognize them.

So it is perhaps not a shock that plague should have presented us with this recognition in such an accelerated way; that it should have intimated, because it finally proved, an equality that we still find so hard to believe. The conviction that arrived at the deathbed becomes less sure as the deathbed becomes a memory—and a memory so awful that we would prefer, indeed long, to forget it. And liberation seems less imperative as our mortality becomes less urgent and as its power to transform our own lives seems less tangible. So we find our will fading and our conviction weak. I wonder whether, for my generation, it is still too late for the liberation we dream of. For us, the conflict between joy and dignity was constructed long ago, and will never be fully unraveled. It happened the moment we internalized that we were homosexual, because at the same moment we knew that we would never be able to have the kind of relationship our parents took for granted. We knew then that a recognized love, an accepted and supported love, was unavailable to us, and a wall rose up inside.

For that reason, of course, marriage itself assumes an intensity of response among my own generation that others may not be able to feel far less comprehend. "Why on earth would you want the right to marry?" is a question that can only come from someone who has never for a second presumed he didn't already have it. And the visceral response to marriage among homosexuals can range from an instinctual loathing to a ridiculous idealization. But it is all part of the same thing, that exquisite sense of being at the heart of the family and yet excluded from it, the recipient of an acceptance that is premised on a rejection. And the sense of having lived through an experience that proved beyond a shadow of a doubt that we deserved an equality yet for a while robbed us of the energy and focus to achieve it.

LAST, THE THINGS I want to remember.

In the last eighteen months, I have begun to believe I will live a normal life. By normal, of course, I don't mean without complications. I take twenty-seven pills a day. At first, they were large, cold pills I kept in the refrigerator, pills that, every day, would send my legs buckling under me and throw me into a sudden, incapacitated sleep every afternoon. And then they were chalky tablets that stuck in the throat, tablets that so nauseated my stomach that I dry-vomited before most meals. But normal in the sense that mortality, or at least the insistence of mortality, doesn't hold my face to the wall every day. I mean I live with the expectation that life is not immediately fragile; that if I push it, it will not break.

It is a strange feeling, this, and a little hard to communicate. When you have spent several years girding yourself for the possibility of death, it is not so easy to gird yourself instead for the possibility of life. What you expect to greet with the euphoria of victory comes instead like the slow withdrawal of an excuse. And you resist it. The extremity with which you approached each day turns into a banality, a banality that refuses to understand or even appreciate the experience you have just gone through.

Of course, I remember feeling this banality before, and I remember the day it ended. I remember the doctor offering me a couple of pieces of candy before we walked back into his office and he fumbled a way of telling me. I've thought about that moment a lot in the past few months. When my doctor called a year and a half ago to tell me that my viral load was now undetectable, part of me wanted to feel as if that first moment of mortality had been erased. But of course, that moment can never be erased. And not simply because I cannot dare hope that one day the virus might be wiped completely from my system, but because some experiences can never be erased. Blurred, perhaps, and distant, but never gone for good.

And in fact, beneath the sudden exhilaration, part of me also wants to keep the moment alive, since it allowed me to see things that I had never been able to see before.

I saw, to begin with, that I was still ashamed. Even then—even in me, someone who had thought and worked and struggled to banish the stigma and the guilt and the fear of my homosexuality—I instinctively interpreted this illness as something that I deserved. Its arrival obliterated all that carefully constructed confidence in my own self-worth. It showed me in a flash how so much of that achievement had been illusory—how, in a pinch, I still loathed and feared an inextricable part of who I was.

The diagnosis was so easily analogized to my sexuality not simply because of how I got it, but also because it was so confoundingly elusive. Until I started to take the medications, I felt no sickness. I had no symptoms. There was nothing tangible against which I could fight—no perceptible, physical ailment which medicine could treat. So it seemed less like an illness than some amorphous, if devastating, condition of life. Suddenly, it existed like my homosexuality had always existed, as something no one from the outside could glean, something I alone could know, and something that always promised a future calamity.

For days after my diagnosis, I went through periodic, involuntary, shaking spasms. My head literally sank onto my chest; I found it hard to look up or see where I was going. The fear of death and sense of failure—and the knowledge that there was nothing I could do to escape this awareness—kept me staring at the sidewalk. At night, asleep, exhaustion gave way to anxiety as panic woke me up. And then, one morning, a couple of weeks later, after walking with a friend to get some coffee and muffins for breakfast, I realized in the first few sips of coffee, that for a few short seconds of physical pleasure, I had actually forgotten what had just happened to me. I realized then that it was going to be possible to forget, that the human mind could find a way to absorb the knowledge that we are going to die and yet continue to live as if we are not. I experienced in some awful, concentrated fashion what I used to know by instinct.

From then on, I suppose, I began the journey back. I realized that this diagnosis was no different in kind than the diagnosis every mortal being lives with—only different in degree. By larger and larger measures, I began to see the condition not as something constricting but as something liberating—liberating because it forced me to confront more profoundly than ever before whether or not my sexuality was something shameful (I became convinced that it was not), and liberating because an awareness of the inevitability of death is always the surest way to an awareness of the tangibility of life.

And unlike so many others who are told they are going to die, and so many people who had been told they were HIV-positive before me, I had time and health and life ahead. In one way, as I still lost friend after friend, and as others lived with griefs that would never be expunged, I experienced this with a certain amount of guilt. But also, as someone graced by the awareness of a fatal disease but not of its fatality, a heightened sense of the possibilities of living. I realized I could do what I wanted to do, write what I wanted to write, be with the people I wanted to be with. So I wrote a book with a calm I had never felt before about a truth I had only belatedly come to believe. The date I inscribed in its preface was two years to the day since my diagnosis: a first weapon against the virus, and a homage to its powers of persuasion.

Not that there weren't moments when the whole idea of liberation with HIV seemed preposterous. My thirtieth birthday remains in my mind the bleakest day I can remember. I was on Cape Cod, six weeks after my diagnosis, and naively confident that the worst was over. But shock has a habit of creeping up on you, and the bad news of the previous month hadn't been confined to me. One of my closest friends, Patrick, had just come down with pneumocystis, an AIDS-related pneumonia; the man I'd fallen in love with that previous winter had found out he was positive three weeks after I did (and was bedridden with viral meningitis); and, to round out the news, in the same month, my mother had been hospitalized with bipolar depression and was undergoing intense medical therapy in England. Because of a transition in my immigration status, my lawyer told me I could not visit her. It was not, to put it mildly, a great time in my life.

So I had left for Cape Cod, a place that has always drawn me at times of stress. I took a walk the morning of my birthday, and as I trekked alone across the dunes at the tip of the peninsula, I suddenly found myself stopping dead. It was about 11:30 on a hot and cloudless morning. I sat down in the sand. It's hard now to explain what was going through my mind at the time. I suppose the best way I can express it is to say that for the first time in my life, like a swift and unexpected shift in the weather, the option of real doubt presented itself to me. It wasn't that I suddenly entertained the idea that God did not exist—such a thought still strikes me as absurd. It was that, for the first time in my life, as I saw the sheer bloody damage done to good people around me, it occurred to me that God was evil. And not evil in some broad generic way, but in an intimate and specific way, a designed way.

This plague, I reflected, had not really struck the high and the low. It had singled out those already struggling and punished them some more; it had given their enemies further ammunition to stigmatize and ignore them; it could have been conceived precisely to ensure that those already fortunate and protected would be preserved. There was self-pity and a certain narcissism in these thoughts, I realized, but there was also a righteous and alarming anger. Those ten minutes were among the loneliest in my life.

And then the feeling lifted. I have no idea how, or why, or where from. It just lifted out of my mind. Like those inexplicable transcendent moments a month or so before, I was aware of this occurring not because of me but somehow in spite of me. It had something to do, I suppose, with an involuntary awareness that such doubts, and doubts of such depth, were, in fact, the ultimate temptation, and that such a temptation was really another word for despair. And, for reasons I still don't understand, I found it impossible to despair.

It was only then perhaps that I realized how much faith I had—or perhaps, more accurately, only then that I actually had it. What I thought had been faith had been, in fact, merely the impression of belief, or the habit of belief, or the memory of belief. So I saw what Milton meant when he said that the virtue that has never known vice was in fact a false virtue, possessed, in his memorable phrase, of an excremental whiteness, without color and texture and grip. Faith, too, without this kind of doubt was, I saw, a faded imprint, not the painting itself. And so I got up out of the sand, and strapped my knapsack to my shoulders, and headed out toward the sea.

I promised a friend of mine at the time, someone in exactly the same boat as I was, that when all of this was over, when we had become used to the idea of HIV as a manageable condition, when the trauma had subsided, and the subject and its attendant grief had become a universal bore, we would never allow ourselves to forget just how truly frightening it was. But, of course, we did forget. We forgot within days of a good blood report, and within hours of a sleepless night. And we forgot so blissfully when the lab data arrived that told us that the virus had disappeared from measurement, and when for a few hours it was hard to remember anything but the sheer, blinding thrill of being free of it, or even able to contemplate being free of it.

And then something strange happened. As if on some bizarre cue, a week or so after discovering that my virus was "undetectable," I found myself sinking into a yawning depression, finding it hard to get up in the morning, harder still to contemplate the simple tasks of making a living, or engaging a world—gay and straight—oblivious to what I had just seen or witnessed. I withdrew even further from company, finding it increasingly crippling to go out into the world or engage the old habits of work and gossip and ambition. Some call this survivor guilt, although it didn't feel like guilt. I was glad beyond measure to be alive, to be well, to be here; but the sadness still surrounded me like a blanket, muffling everything. The indicatives of plague, I realized, were turning slowly back into subjunctives, the duties into doubts, and there was no easy out.

As a friend of mine—another survivor—put it, I felt, in some strange way, post-everything. Post-plague, post-death, post-mortality, post-career, post-fear; even the very memories of plague sent my mind into a dulling tiredness. Sometimes I found myself making daily decisions with complete detachment and faint nausea, because no other feelings were available to me. I would catch myself with other survivors and think, for some strange moment, that nothing had happened at all, that it was still some kind of illusion. One night, I was in a familiar bar, a bar I had been in many times with Patrick and with Greg Scott, and suddenly Greg was there again, fit and lean and well and scamming on everyone and everything around him. And we laughed and drank beer, as we had done many times before, and as I went to the restroom and leaned over the urinal, I found myself staring at the wall and asking myself, in the most absurdly literal way, why Pat wasn't there anymore; and where he had gone; and why, in what seemed like a sudden time warp, some of us were around and some of us were not. It was not a memory, or a regret. It was a puzzlement. A numbing, deadening, saddening puzzlement.

Maybe that puzzlement is something we should always feel but cannot bring ourselves to. Maybe feeling it as a deadening, draining background to my days is something I should think of as a gift, a gift of a heightened sense of what is actually real, and what I cannot understand. And when it comes too suddenly or with too much insistence, I try to remember, although I resist remembering, how for a precious short time, like so many other positive people, I sensed that the key to living was not a concentration on fighting the mechanics of the disease (although that was essential) or fighting the mechanics of life (although that is inevitable), but an indifference to both their imponderables. In order to survive mentally, I had had to find a place within myself where plague couldn't get me, where success or failure in such a battle were of equal consequence. This was not an easy task. It required resisting the emotional satisfaction of being cured and the emotional closure of death itself, resisting the safety of knowing and the relief of not knowing. But in that, of course, it resembled merely what we all go through every day. Living, I discovered for the second, but really the first, time, is not about resolution; it is about the place where plague can't get you.

Only once or twice did I find that place, but now I live in the knowledge of its existence. So will, perhaps, a generation.

2. VIRTUALLY ABNORMAL

> They fuck you up, your mum and dad,
> They may not mean to, but they do . . .
> —Philip Larkin, *This Be the Verse*

"WHY CAN'T YOU BE more *normal*?" my father once yelled at his neurotic, teenage son. "Well, what's normal?" I hurled back. It was a good question, however defensively yelled; and still is. During the plague, it became perhaps more pressing than ever. "The poor homosexuals," Patrick Buchanan memorably wrote. "They declared war on nature and now nature has taken its revenge." As the epidemic continued its onslaught, and as the human horror of its path through the lives of hundreds of thousands of gay men became clearer, the question receded. It became offensive, even obscene, to raise the question of the "normality" of people in such distress, to disregard what they so obviously had in common with everyone else—fear, family, isolation, death—from what resiliently set them apart.

But as a decade passed, and as the plague ebbed, the question that had never been fully answered, the question, indeed, that had never been fully and thoroughly asked, revived. On the left, an ancient squabble broke out—between those who feared that continued promiscuity could put yet another generation of gay men in mortal danger and those who defended and even celebrated that promiscuity as somehow definitive of what it was to be gay. And on the right, after a decade of defensive posturing, and quizzical silence, and stunning political retreat on the homosexual question, a decision was clearly made.

An old but trusty theory was resurrected to define the essential pathology of homosexuality. At the biggest conference organized by the right to address the homosexual question ever, the first day was devoted to a defense of what they call "reparative" psychoanalytic therapy for homosexuals. In the very brochure for the conference, homosexuality was described as a "disease." As a cure for HIV approached, the right did what it could to advance the notion of a cure for homosexuality itself.

As AIDS receded, in other words, the fundamental question of normality revived again. And the apostles of abnormality had a field day. Indeed, by linking homosexuality intrinsically to sexual pathology, the leaders of the fundamentalist right formed a strange echo to the shrill rhetoric of the "queer" left. Homosexuality became defined again as a profound malfunction, a subversive behavior, and a pathological way of life. The question was merely whether it should be celebrated or cured.

In many ways, of course, both extremes were marginal to the lives and thoughts of most Americans, gay and straight. But by fastening onto the fundamental issue of normality, both extremes, nevertheless, were at least more honest and often more interesting than many in between. By insisting that until this profound issue was fully grappled with, no meaningful cultural compromise could be reached, both sides reiterated a truth it would have been more convenient and certainly less painful to ignore.

And publicly, of course, most homosexuals do ignore it. They claim (rightly) that it is politically irrelevant, and dismiss (understandably) the indignity of defending themselves from charges of dysfunction. And yet, behind the public postures, few homosexuals, in reality, are truly ambivalent to the issue of normality. Indeed, in almost every conversation between gay people, especially those caught in the social transformation that is now happening, the issue looms. Degrees of effeminacy or masculinity are calibrated with as much precision as skin color is among many blacks. If a relationship fails, there is a temptation to generalize its failures not simply to human frailty but to homosexual frailty. Like so many other minorities, this particular minority is obsessed with its relationship with the other, with hazarding some kind of compromise between normality and deviance. Whether to wear a tie or grow a beard, to put on a dress or wear some lipstick: tiny, daily rituals that fit routinely into every heterosexual's life become tiny signposts for the homosexual, internal and external signals about where normal ends and life begins.

At times, this permanent self-analysis cripples a person, which is why many homosexuals drift to the extremes of normal or abnormal identity and find it hard to find a stable center in between. After all, it is hard to engage in a permanent inquiry into what is psychologically healthy without putting one's own emotional balance at risk. The gay child or adolescent, or the fledgling gay adult, is so assailed by social disdain that she can rarely afford the vulnerability that complete honesty requires. It's not as if, in most cases, she can take time out from her life to figure out who she is; she has to figure it out *while* she lives, and while her parents and friends, colleagues and church, siblings and lovers, impose a willful definition of normality upon her. And when she does engage in the search—in the quiet moments stolen from social interaction—she has to do so against the tide of shame that pushes her as powerfully inward as pride pushes her powerfully outward. And these impulses can make for a crippling combination. Shame forces you prematurely to run away from yourself; pride forces you prematurely to expose yourself. Most gay lives, I'm afraid, are full of an embarrassing abundance of both.

We're told, of course, that even framing the question this way is a symptom of self-loathing; and you can see why. It is often painful, sometimes intolerably so, to put oneself under the mental knife, to start an inquiry not knowing whether one's own deepest identity will end up pathologized. It's like being conscious during surgery. But, then, isn't any truly examined life supposed to be like this? We have gotten too used to the idea that thinking should always defer to sensitivity, that identity trumps reality, that identity *is* reality. But it is perhaps more often true that the more offended one's identity is, the closer one is to a genuine intellectual and experiential risk. And all the most interesting questions have the potential to inflict pain.

I avoided this pain for a long time, and I make no apologies for doing so. Living was precarious enough without self-excision. But it became unavoidable with my diagnosis. I said earlier that my first reaction to learning I was HIV-positive was a powerful sense that I had somehow deserved it, that it was a fitting punishment for a life lived, at its deepest, emotional level, against the norm. I don't mean that I felt I'd risked infection wantonly, that my infection was the punishment for breaking the sexual rules in an epidemic. I had, in fact, never had unprotected anal inter-course before my infection. In some ways, it would have been more of a relief if I had. I could have beaten myself up for a stupid lapse, and isolated the sense of failure and shame I felt. Instead, the sense of punishment that returned with such a vengeance was oppressively inchoate and pervasive and profound. If it couldn't be related to a single mistake, then what could it be related to? It brought to the surface again every simmering anxiety I had ever felt about the normality of my life, and the morality of my loves. It was as if every small step I'd ever made toward being honest and open and self-confident in my sexual and emotional life had been erased in one lab report. I was back, graphically and clarifyingly, to square one.

WHICH IS WHY, perhaps, I found myself reading Freud. Oddly enough, I had already been embarked on a pro-gram of psychotherapy for some time, and why I had avoided reading the master himself is no doubt a good subject in itself for analysis. Still, for whatever reason, it wasn't until the threat of death receded that I felt strong enough to ask the questions that many gay men and women do not particularly want to ask at all. And those questions relate to the deepest issues of identity and health. Am I normal or not? And what follows from either of the possible answers to that question?

The great merit of the psychoanalytic literature on homosexuality is that it addresses this unabashedly. Indeed, apart from relatively recent, and inconclusive, scientific inquiries, it's the *only* discourse that addresses it unabashedly. You can ransack the theologians for a nuanced view as to what the origins or meaning of homosexuality might actually be, and come away with remarkably thin gruel. Or indeed, listen to most of the political discussants and find either an assumption that obviously there is nothing wrong with homosexuality, or an assumption that obviously there is nothing right. Theorists on the right are too busy asserting that homosexuality is wrong to explain at any length why it occurs, and theorists on the left are too busy explaining why the whole concept of normal is meaningless to figure out how homosexuality arises. The vast terrain in between lies still oddly unexplored—the one side abandoning it for fear of seeming racked with self-loathing, the other side abandoning it for fear of seeming like bigots.

So psychoanalysis is not only a good place to start to examine the normality of homosexuality. In many ways, in the realm of the humanities, it is the most interesting place to start. And the range of responses to the question is larger than one might, at first blush, imagine—from Freud's skeptical insights in the early part of this century to the magisterial condemnations of homosexual pathology in the 1950s to the humane defenses of homosexual normality in the 1990s. What this discourse does is what we all intuitively want to do—confront homosexuality's origins in the natural order of gender, procreation and love. For me, it formed another way to think about the teleology of homosexuality, to answer the question "What are homosexuals for?" in a nonpolitical but vital way. For psychoanalysis, while often eschewing—

certainly in its early days—a reductionist biological destiny for humankind, is nonetheless resistant to abandoning a concept of normality altogether. The tradition, after all, is premised on an attempt to explain and then therapize the conflicts that create unhappiness. It cannot avoid, then, normalizing the natural happiness it attempts to bring about. And in this process, homosexuality has always been a revealing and resilient stumbling block.

In reading Freud, the thing that most struck me was his attempt to understand, rather than resolve, the question of homosexuality. Perhaps the most surprising quality of his work is its modesty. Freud questions, but he rarely answers; he puzzles, but he seldom asserts. To read him today is to be awed by the contrast with many of his current acolytes. In one of the bizarrest twists of contemporary politics, it is those with the fiercest theological convictions—the fundamentalist right—who now most frequently invoke this most quizzical and frustrating of intellectuals. And it's only by reading Freud himself that one begins fully to appreciate the irony.

Freud first subverts the category. There is, he suggests, no homosexual. There are only homosexuals divided into three main categories: "absolute inverts," "amphigenic inverts," and "contingent inverts." Amphigenics are what we would now call bisexuals, people whose "sexual objects may equally well be of their own or of the opposite sex." Contingents are those who have sexual relations with the same sex merely for want of an alternative: prisoners, English schoolboys, etc. Only "absolute inverts" qualify as essential homosexuals. But even here, Freud eschews the certainty of modern gay rights advocates; it is not a rigid identity, at least not in many. And it can provoke a variety of responses: comfort, panic, neurosis, or calm.

Freud is not threatened intellectually by these possibilities, or even by their potential conflicts. Take his view of the question as to whether homosexuality is "innate." For Freud, it is clear that it may not be innate for some, but it clearly is for others: "The evidence for it rests upon assurances given by [inverts] that at no time in their lives has their sexual instinct shown any sign of taking another course." He acknowledges that some observers held that some homosexuals may have "acquired" their homosexuality by early experience and that there was some evidence that homosexual orientation could be removed by hypnosis, "which would be astonishing in an innate characteristic." Nonetheless, Freud appears to be convinced that such evidence was "completely countered by the reflection that many people are subject to the same sexual influences (e.g., to seduction or mutual masturbation, which may occur in early youth) without becoming inverted or without remaining so permanently." For Freud, some complex combination of "innateness" and "environment" is obviously at work here, and it is likely to vary widely from case to case. Or as he puts it, "We are therefore forced to a suspicion that the choice between 'innate' and 'acquired' is not an exclusive one or that it does not cover all the issues involved in aversion." It's a classic Freudian phrase that: "forced to a suspicion."

And from early paragraphs to later footnotes, Freud forces us toward a dozen other suspicions. For Freud, startlingly enough, the evidence for the "normality" of homosexuality is abundant. Homosexuality, he observes, is not necessarily related to any social or psychological malfunction, and it is certainly unrelated to the nineteenth-century notion of "degeneracy"; "Inversion is found in people who exhibit no other serious deviations from the normal," he notes. "It is similarly found in people whose efficiency is unimpaired, and who are indeed distinguished by specially high intellectual development and ethical culture." Unlike many of his subsequent followers, Freud is also aware of the problem of psychoanalysts generalizing from their patient population, a group of people who naturally tend to be disturbed, psychologically troubled, and likely to be in conflict with their sexual identity, whatever it is. "It must be borne in mind," he writes, "that hitherto only a single type of invert has been submitted to psychoanalysis—persons whose sexual activity is in general stunted and the residue of which is manifested as inversion." He leaves open the possibility of an alternative, healthy homosexuality, one which betrayed no marks of conflict or dysfunction, and one with which modern psychoanalysts were unlikely to come in contact. After all, it had flourished before: "Account must be taken of the fact that inversion was a frequent phenomenon—one might almost say an institution charged with important functions, among the peoples of antiquity at the height of their civilization."

Effeminacy among homosexuals is a myth, Freud notices. On the contrary, "the most perfect psychic manliness may be united with the inversion." One theory, he notes, holds that "the sexual object of an invert is the opposite of that of a normal person. An inverted man, it holds, is like a woman in being subject to the charm that proceeds from masculine attributes both physical and mental: he feels he is a woman in search of a man. But however well this applies to quite a number of inverts, it is, nevertheless, far from revealing a universal characteristic of inversion. There can be no doubt that a large proportion of male inverts retain the mental quality of masculinity, that they possess relatively few of the secondary characters of the opposite sex and that what they look for in their sexual object are in fact feminine traits." For Freud, this is a function of a constitutional, universal bisexuality, which could be resolved homosexually, heterosexually, or ambiguously. The point, he seems to argue, is to marvel at the variety of human sexual and emotional experience, and to *infer* malfunction or conflict or sickness if it occurred in the many expressions of that variety, but not to mistake diversity for disorder.

So homosexuality, for Freud, was never inherently pathological or sick. Quite the reverse. "I am . . . of the firm conviction," he famously wrote to the newspaper *Die Zeit* in 1905, "that homosexuals must not be treated as sick people . . . Wouldn't that oblige us to characterize as sick many great thinkers and scholars . . . whom we admire precisely because of their mental health? Homosexual persons are not sick. They also do not belong in a court of law!" And if homosexuality was not a sickness, then it followed that it could not be cured. Freud's belief that a psychoanalytic cure of homosexuality was extremely unlikely and ill-conceived was to be obscured by generations of (particularly American) psychoanalysts, whose first response to the phenomenon of homosexuality was to seek to cure it. So it's worth repeating Freud's words: "In actual numbers, the successes achieved by psychoanalytic treatment of ... homosexuality ... are not very striking ... In general, to undertake to convert a fully developed homosexual into a heterosexual is not much more promising than to do the reverse."

This equation of homosexuality and heterosexuality—putting them on the same plane with regard to adult emotional and sexual function—is particularly striking when read today. Freud was in no uncertain terms a human assimilationist, reluctant to obscure a common humanity under a rubric of sexual identity. "Psychoanalytic research very strongly opposes the attempt to separate homosexuals from other persons as a group of a special nature," he wrote. "In the psychoanalytic sense the exclusive interest of the man for the woman is also a problem requiring an explanation, and is not something that is self-evident."

So his attitude toward psychoanalytic treatment of homosexuality was, at best, skeptical. His most remarkable statement to this effect is now a celebrated document. It took the form of a letter to the American mother of a homosexual son. The woman had written Freud to ask for his advice about what to do about her gay son. She was so uncomfortable with the fact that she couldn't even bring herself to use the term "homosexual." And it was with her reticence that Freud first took issue:

> I gather from your letter that your son is a homosexual. I am most impressed by the fact that you do not mention this term yourself in your information about him. May I question you, why do you avoid it?

Homosexuality is assuredly no advantage, but it is nothing to be ashamed of, no vice, no degradation, it cannot be classified as an illness; we consider it to be a variation of the sexual function produced by a certain arrest of sexual development . . . By asking me if I can help, you mean, I suppose, if I can abolish homosexuality and make normal heterosexuality take its place. The answer is, in a general way, we cannot promise to achieve it. In a certain number of cases we succeed in developing the blighted germs of heterosexual tendencies which are present in every homosexual, in the majority of cases it is no more possible. It is a question of the quality and the age of the individual . . . What analysis can do for your son runs in a different line. If he is unhappy, neurotic, torn by conflicts, inhibited in his social life, analysis may bring him harmony, peace of mind, full efficiency whether he remains a homosexual, or gets changed . . .

For the early part of this century, it is a remarkable testimony. And yet in the middle of this extraordinary document of acceptance, there is that telling phrase: "a certain arrest of sexual development." And there is also that term which Freud used to describe the phenomenon in the first place: "invert." It is, to be sure, distinguished from "pervert." For Freud, homosexuality was not necessarily a perversion, a turning away from sexual union with another human being, a fixation with or attraction to a part of a person, or a thing, rather than a sexual and emotional engagement with a complete and fulfilling other. It was perfectly possible, Freud seemed to believe, for an invert to achieve a full and fulfilling relationship, sexual and emotional, with another man. But he was nonetheless still an invert, somehow not turned away from sexual union but turned *inward* toward union with a part of himself, in what might appear to be a manifestation of narcissism. In other words, at the same time that Freud seemed to support the complete normality of homosexuality, he described it in such a way that it appears to be an aberration or a problem. What, one wonders, did Freud really mean by such a paradox?

The answer is, perhaps predictably, complex. There seem, according to Freud, to be three primary ways in which a child grows up to be a homosexual.* In crude terms, they result from resolving what Freud called the Oedipus complex in ways different from the most common. The Oedipus complex, one recalls, occurs at that period in a child's development when his early, complete identification with his mother, and primal sexual yearning for her, collides with an awareness that sexual union with his mother is forbidden. (For Freud, all infants are what he called "polymorphously perverse.") So the child detaches from the mother and later reattaches his libido,

---

*I am not a trained psychoanalyst, so what follows is a layman's best interpretation of Freud's own writing, especially his *Three Essays on the Theory of Sexuality* and several scholarly interpreters of Freud's work (in particular, the classic studies *The Psychoanalytic Theory of Male Homosexuality*, by Kenneth Lewes; *Homosexuality and American Psychiatry*, by Ronald Bayer; and *Male Homosexuality*, by Richard C. Friedman).

after a period of sexual latency, to a mother substitute, in the form of other women.

In boys who later become homosexuals, something happens, according to Freud, to arrest this development. In one scenario, the mother's attachment to the boy is abnormally intense and leads the child to ascribe much of the force of this attachment to his maleness, in the form of his penis. When the time comes for him to realize that his mother is actually a separate being and also of a different gender, his trauma is therefore even greater than that of a pre-heterosexual boy. He is particularly horrified at the possibility that his mother is without a penis, and subsequently recoils in fear at any sign of female genitalia. Thus, his sexual desire turns ineluctably inward (hence "invert") toward people like himself (with a penis) and, after his own period of latency, attaches to other men. It seems, in layspeak, as if the child is so devoted to his mother that he cannot separate from her at the Oedipal stage, and yet cannot either accept his longing for her. So he retreats into an autoeroticism which is no rival for her love. In later life, he therefore hovers between a narcissistic urge and the human need for another's love and sexual interest: "The choice is towards a narcissistic object which is readier at hand and easier to put into effect than movement towards the opposite sex." So he gravitates toward other men, men who cannot satisfy either his desire to unite fully with another being or his desire to be fully satisfied with union with himself.

In a second scenario, the child again overattaches to his mother, but another form of development ensues. Inverts of this second type, in Freud's words, subsequently "identify themselves with a woman and take *themselves* as their sexual object. That is to say, they proceed from a narcissistic basis, and look for a young man who resembles themselves and whom *they* may love as their mother loved *them*." In this formulation, the homosexual child thinks of himself as a woman, like his mother, and enmeshes his ego with hers. His loving, early bond with his mother is so intense, so gratifying, so enveloping, that he seeks to re-create it in later life in the only way he can as a man, which is by adopting the persona and role of his own mother as his own. In the words of Freud scholar Kenneth Lewes, the child is therefore "able to continue loving his mother in himself, and simultaneously to be loved himself. Where once he was loved, he will now love, turning passive into active."

And then there's a third possibility. It is that, for some reason, a boy's early masculine identification with his father is jolted by some predisposition, event, or Oedipal trauma into a more intense desire to be loved by the father and penetrated by him. This may commonly be caused by a father's rejection, or cruelty, or indifference. So in almost a reverse of overidentification with the mother, the child experiences an overidentification with the father, and, instead of developing to model his life on his father's, the child, separated from the person whom he longs for, seeks rather to be sexually united with him. In one case, Freud saw this development as a consequence of a boy's being seduced by an older sister, turning the boy into a "passive" sexual object, and therefore leading him to seek sexual satisfaction through a passive interaction with an active male; in others, it seems to have been set up by a predisposition to passivity, which subsequently found expression in a passive sexual relationship with the male figure. In these various paths to homosexuality, a longing for the father is a key sexual element, a longing that could have one or several causes.

With regard to female homosexuality, Freud's inquiries are less extensive, but remarkably similar. Pre-lesbian children and girls are, it seems, equally drawn into an intense relationship with their mother, exhibit a strong reluctance to separate from her during the Oedipal phase, and develop an intense resentment of the father for his love relationship with the mother. This resentment leads to a more general resentment of men altogether, and an avoidance of those male-female relationships which remind the child of the jealous pain she suffered at the thought of her mother's "infidelity." Freud thus saw a lesbian's sexual orientation as "probably a direct and unchanged continuation of an infantile fixation on her mother." What's interesting about Freud's discussion of this topic in his 1920 monograph, "Psychogenesis of a Case of Homosexuality in a Woman," is that it was the occasion for his expressing his belief more strongly than elsewhere in the constitutional nature of homosexuality. The psychological causes of lesbianism, after all, were experiences—resentment of the father, closeness to mother—that many children undergo without apparent trauma. Something prior to experience, Freud suggests, must predispose a pre-lesbian child to experience this trauma and then to become sexually and emotionally oriented to other women.

Reading Freud as a layman today is to be struck both by how absurd some of his arguments seem—all that obsession with penises—but also how intuitively close to reality his arguments appear. For all of Freud's obvious failings, I defy any honest homosexual to read Freud's work in this area and not find something worth pondering about his own development or the associations of his own desire. This is true for heterosexuals too, of course, whose Oedipal complex is resolved just as traumatically, and whose adult longings echo equally with the sounds of their earliest feelings.

But the trouble with these tantalizing analyses, of course, is that they are as impossible to verify as they are to dismiss. Perhaps what Freud does most usefully, then, is to place squarely on the table the very concept of normality with regard to the homosexual—without an apparent animus or defensiveness. Homosexuality, for Freud, seems to be neither normal development, in the sense that it doesn't affect the overwhelming majority of people. Nor is it optimal, in the sense that, somehow, despite what Freud understood to be an early capacity to be sexually attracted to virtually anything (male and female), human beings are brought to the fullest stage of development, he seems to believe, by resolving their Oedipal crises by a final attachment to a member of the opposite sex.

So the resolution of the homosexual Oedipal conflict is, for Freud, suboptimal, arrested, incomplete. And yet at same time the homosexual is neither a pervert nor a fetishist; his desire is not necessarily for an object that is incomplete or for a sexual engagement that is partial. And his development in some respects is completely interchangeable with the heterosexual's, except for the switch in the gender of the object of desire. And although narcissism seems, for Freud, to be connected to some forms of homosexual development, thus rendering the homosexual at a disadvantage in his future relations, it is not connected with all of them.

To add to this dizzying variety of interpretations, it seems at times as if Freud is also deliberately undermining the possible consequences of his argument, first clearly normalizing heterosexuality and then subsequently equating the two sexual orientations with startling frankness. After all, if one is to infer what is normal from what is embedded most deeply in human identity, then, for Freud, it is clear that bisexuality is the norm, and that both heterosexuality and homosexuality demand equally searching explanations: "Psychoanalysis considers that a choice of an object independently of its sex—freedom to range equally over male and female objects—as it is found in childhood, in primitive states of society and early periods of history, is the original basis from which, as a result of restriction in one direction or the other, both the normal and the inverted types develop. Thus from the point of view of psychoanalysis the exclusive sexual interest felt by men for women is also a problem that needs elucidating and is not a self-evident fact based upon an attraction that is ultimately of a chemical nature." And yet, at the same time, one group is defined by the term "invert"; the other group is defined by nothing, except their membership in the human race.

*

HOW DO WE BEGIN to make sense of this? One way, perhaps, is to attempt to read out of Freud all those qualifica-
tions to the normality of homosexuality and retrofit him
for a more contemporary, tolerant analysis. And this is
exactly what many modern gay-friendly psychoanalysts
have attempted to do. But just as interesting—and arguably more revealing—is to attempt to do the opposite:
to try to resolve Freud's ambivalence into a full-scale
argument for the abnormality and pathology of homosexuality, and then to see what remains to be explained or
understood. One way, after all, of understanding the am-
biguous nature of homosexuality is to try to abolish the
ambiguity; to describe it, in Freud's own terms, as an irre-
deemably abnormal and disordered condition; and to
take all steps necessary to eradicate it.

For good or ill, this particular path is not a new one. In
many ways, Freud's followers did it for us, pathologizing
homosexuality in the 1940s and 1950s with a rigor and
determination typical of the certainty of psychiatry's
glory days. And despite the American Psychiatric Association's dramatic change of heart in 1973, when, under intense political pressure, it removed homosexuality from
its official list of psychiatric disorders, many psychoanalysts still quietly view homosexuality as a suboptimal
form of emotional and sexual functioning and seek
through therapy either to alleviate or, in some cases, to
"cure" it.

Alas, only a few brave souls are prepared to make this

bracing case in public, while it still hovers in the public (and gay) consciousness like the theory that dare not speak its name. There's a human reason, of course, for this taboo. To enter the world of the "reparative" therapists is, in many ways, a gay man's worst nightmare, and few heterosexuals who aren't themselves consumed personally with the issue would wish to inflict such trauma on the homosexuals they know or care about. And indeed, it's hard for a gay man to read the articles and books of the "reparative therapists," or to listen to their speeches, without hearing the taunts of the playground echoing in their ears, taunts that are now armored with the authority of "experts."

Still, it's not hard to understand the resilience and appeal of the theory. It has the tone of scientific authority in an area which has for so long been saturated with confusion; and the mixture of judgment and compassion in the writings of the reparative therapists, their promise of pain and release, strikes deep, redemptive, and painful chords in the homosexual psyche. At some level, perhaps, the lure of this kind of psychoanalysis for the homosexual is a little like the lure of fundamentalist religion, because it identifies with devastating clarity the often difficult contours of a homosexual life and then offers, in precise calibration with its description, a form of self-erasing escape. Above all, it provides an explanation, a way out, a release from the frustrating twilight world into which the gay man has been thrust since his earliest consciousness.

I once tried to buy one of the therapists' books from a gay bookstore in Washington, D.C. It's a store known to stock virtually anything on the subject of homosexuality, and, indeed, it had the book catalogued in its computer. But next to the title was the simple moniker: "bad." Not "out of stock" or "out of print." Merely "bad." It was deemed so offensive, so dangerous, that even a bookstore censored it. The hostility and fear have a long pedigree. When the protests against reparative therapy climaxed in the 1970s, gay activists accused its practitioners of trying to commit homosexual "genocide." Such were the feelings that reparative therapy generated, and understandably so. But the extremity of the opposition seems in retrospect somewhat defensive. Why, after all, be afraid of a genocide, if you are convinced your tormentors are firing blanks?

Reading some of the reparative therapists, however, is convincing evidence that, whatever their serious arguments, the hostility they provoke is often well deserved. Despite protestations that they are motivated by compassion for homosexuals trapped in what they call "the lifestyle," some feel free to vent what could reasonably be seen at times as a thinly veiled incitement to hatred. Charles Socarides, for example, the most prolific and prominent of the reparative therapists, has routinely elided pedophilia with homosexuality. In a speech given to the 1995 conference of the National Association for Research and Therapy of Homosexuality (NARTH), for example, he proclaimed that militant homosexuals "have told us, 'We're here. We're queer. And we're coming after your children.' How much more do we need to know?"

In his most recent book, *Homosexuality: A Freedom Too Far,* Socarides accused homosexuals of spreading HIV and took the example of mass-murderer Jeffrey Dahmer as merely an extreme version of a common homosexual type, different from other homosexuals only in degree, not in kind. He analogized Dahmer's cannibalism with what he described as the average homosexual's erotic impulse to "incorporate" parts of other men's bodies into themselves.

The comparison of gay rights activists with Nazis is also a trope among some NARTH supporters. Again in 1995, a writer published by NARTH, Ray Johnson, thundered against the APA's refusal to recognize reparative therapy: "Whether the zealots joined wear brown shirts, pink triangles, or raise the clenched fist of radical feminism, when professional and scientific organizations embrace their cause, the scientific enterprise dies and is replaced by propaganda and coercion." One of the papers submitted to the 1995 conference went so far as to make the metaphor historical reality. "It was no coincidence that homosexuals were among those who founded the Nazi Party," wrote Scott Lively, a political activist in Oregon. "In fact, the party grew out of a number of groups in Germany which were centers of homosexual activity and activism." As for Nazi persecution of homosexuals, "there is evidence that only the effeminate homosexuals were mistreated under the Nazi regime—and usually at the hands of masculine homosexuals." And those effeminate homosexuals, Lively later remarks, "may have brought on themselves the later wrath of the Nazis" by antagonizing their macho brothers.

These extremist excursions are not typical of the work of all reparative therapists, however, and they do not affect their central psychoanalytic arguments. Still, the fact that they are entertained by one of the movement's leading lights, and that such ideas can be published in NARTH's collected papers, is surely worth noting. It is certainly hard to reconcile the harshness of this rhetoric with the firm and neutral empathy required of professional psychoanalysts. Even taking account of the bruising political wars they have been engaged in, the contrast with Freud's own calm curiosity is stark.

Given these motivations, it might legitimately be asked why one should read or engage these people at all. And the answer is a pretty simple one: bigots can also have arguments. And when their arguments lie behind playground taunts and adult silences, when they drive the shame that refuses to relinquish its hold on even the most self-confident of homosexuals, then the need to understand and engage those arguments becomes even more pressing. And when their case is championed and embraced by an entire wing of the political debate, and by one of the major political parties, when it is echoed even by the Senate Majority Leader, then it is also important, purely for the sake of clarity, to subject that case to further investigation.

And when you do, the Freudian influence (and departure from that influence) becomes clearer. The flesh is put on the master's analytic bones. The reparative therapists' psychoanalytic paradigm of homosexuality is largely the same as the first psychoanalyst's, with some critical adjustments. Here is an attempt at a rough, layman's summary, drawn from the writing of some of the leading reparative therapists and from the officially published papers of NARTH in recent years.

*

FOR MOST OF THE reparative therapists, homosexuality begins with a gender-identity disorder among young children, who experience an overly close relationship with the mother and an overly distant relationship with the father. Ironically, some of these analysts (Socarides in particular) place the critical emergence of pre-homosexual development earlier than Freud did, believing it takes place long before the age of three. And there seems to be a growing consensus among these types that it is the distant relationship with the father that is more instrumental in such a development than an overly close attachment to the mother.

In other words, it is a familiar psychoanalytic version of the vernacular "mommy's boy" or "sissy boy" paradigm. Here's a useful, somewhat typical summary, from the psychotherapist Martin Silverman:

> ... [A] boy is born to a basically depressed mother whose depression may not always be overtly apparent ... She reacts to the birth of a son by investing in him as a means of completing herself, fulfilling her yearnings, and endowing herself with the capacity to feel whole, self-reliant, and protected against the pain of loss, abandonment and unfulfilled need ... She communicates to [her son] from the very beginning that he can remain in her good graces as her loved and cherished child only if he gives up his aspirations to be separate, independent, and differ-

ent . . . The boy reacts by developing early and intense insecurity, ambivalence, and fear of being separate from his mother that approaches the unconscious conviction that he cannot and does not exist apart from his mother . . . The father tends to be passive, helpless, conflicted about his own needfulness and about his own sexual identity. He tends to feel powerless to oppose his wife's insistent dominance of his son's increasing effeminacy. He tends to be under assertive and under aggressive, or given to intense though shortlived, impotent rages, or to alternate between the two . . . [The boy therefore] oscillates between the wish to guard and protect his separate, independent identity and his penis and the need to sacrifice his independent aspirations to hold on to his idealized, all-powerful, all-providing mother.

Thus the boy eventually so identifies with his mother, so absorbs her identity into his, that later sexual interaction with girls or women becomes impossible; and sexual attraction to men becomes second nature. Or, put another way, the boy, wounded by his father's distance, "defensively detaches" from his father. This defensive detachment, in the words of A. Dean Byrd, another reparative therapist, "serves as a protection against hurt from males during childhood. In adulthood, it serves as a barrier to honest intimacy and mutuality between men. The resulting sense of incompleteness fuels a reparative drive or desire to complete oneself. This is manifested in the eroticization of other men, sexualizing that with which the male homosexual is not identified."

Socarides puts the entire syndrome in clear, metaphor-
ical language. The "obligatory homosexual" (Socarides's
version of Freud's "absolute invert")

> had an over-controlling mother and a father who
> was disengaged. I call such a father "abdicating"—
> because he has, for various reasons, forfeited his
> rightful duty as a father. He gave his son no real role
> model, and so his son ended up looking for his mas-
> culinity [elsewhere].*

Later, Socarides's description of the nature of this abnormality is eloquently graphic:

> [Child-rearing] is somewhat like planting a sunflower
> seed. Normally I will see that seed break through the
> earth and develop into a full-grown plant. Only if
> I plant it where it can get no sunlight, or if I fail to

*It is worth mentioning here something that Socarides fails to acknowl-
edge in A Freedom Too Far, which is that his own son is homosexual. In
fact, his son is not merely homosexual but the Clinton administration's
chief political liaison to the gay and lesbian community. This doesn't
reflect on the cogency (or otherwise) of Socarides's arguments, of
course, which deserve examination on their own merits. But it might
help shed some light on the emotional quality of Socarides's writing,
especially since his primary contribution to the literature has been to
argue that the "abdicating father" plays a critical role in a child's emergent homosexuality. It is also worth mentioning that Socarides denied
me legal permission to reproduce here substantive material from his
book because he believes (but I do not) that my statements about him
are "defamatory . . . incorrect, and misinterpretations, and on one occasion reckless and inciting violence" against him.

water it, or if I step on it will it become dangerously deformed.

The reparative therapist's task is therefore to help the patient identify these origins of his homosexual orientation, to re-experience the emotions that created it, and in the course of therapy to reignite the latent heterosexual feelings that the patient can allegedly find within. And note that this applies not just to some disturbed homosexuals but to all of them. Even those who "seem to be well-adjusted" are, in fact, "dangerously deformed." It is worth noting at this point that the reparative therapists, unlike Freud, seem to have an almost complete lack of interest in female homosexuality. Indeed, in four years of NARTH papers, I could find only one account of lesbian development, subsumed in a discussion of gender narcissism. Likewise I could find almost no discussion of lesbianism in many of these therapists' books. This lacuna is one to which I'll return later, since I think it casts an important light on the direction of this particular line of inquiry. Still, male homosexuality provides plenty of biographical material for study, some of it heart-wrenching. Take "Nathan," a patient of one Paul Popper:

> Nathan, who grew up in an extremely violent family in which both his mother and father fought verbally and physically, recalls becoming responsible for keeping his mother happy by being aware of every one of her moods, making her laugh, taking flowers out of garbage cans and presenting them to her,

washing the dishes, and cleaning the house in order to maintain some peace in the home. At age 10, he remembers being severely beaten by his father as punishment for some transgression, a not-unusual occurrence. He remembers walking away from his father with a contemptuous smile on his face, feeling inside that he would never be "touched" by him again. Nathan, who fought with other kids throughout his preadolescence and adolescence and is quite masculine in his carriage and appearance, still identifies men as macho, as fighters, as insensitive and as bullish, and through his therapy has begun to identify how, in all of his relationships, his role was to make others feel comfortable in order to assuage his guilt and his feelings of being condemned.

Nathan went on to date other men, but, apart from one four-month relationship, "during which time, he felt validated and cared for," he could only grab instant intimacy in drunken one-night stands. "After a year, he attends therapy regularly and basks in the narcissistic enjoyment of being accepted and liked. He literally believes that he will go to hell because he has been condemned. This rigid belief has loosened during the last year. He now accepts some of his own imperfections without total self-judgment."

"Andrew's" story is just as vivid:

Andrew describes a scene which he has relived in therapy. He is between the age of three to five. He is in the kitchen with his mother, who is putting on makeup, drying and spraying her hair, sensually exhaling her cigarettes while Andrew is sitting there for hours watching her, mesmerized, listening to her. During this experience the smell of the cigarette smoke and her hairspray are still prevalent and are still clearly available to him as he relives the experience. Between the age of three to five Andrew recalls anxiously waiting for his father to come home, sitting on the curb outside and then walking up to greet him because he was looking forward to his return. He remembers being crushingly disappointed when his father gave him only a perfunctory acknowledgment and went on with his busy, compulsive, rigid lifestyle which excluded Andrew.

The pattern, clearly, is set. Andrew, it turns out, "has lots of memories of being Mom's confidant, listening to her about how men are brutes, insensitive, identifying with her and feeling himself more and more different from men. Andrew recalls that at age eight to nine his father wanted him to work in the garden with him, in the dirt, under the hot sun. He remembers he ran to his mother, who was very sympathetic, washed him up and told him he didn't need to do that." Unlike Nathan, however, Andrew got married. But like Nathan, he retained his homosexual compulsions, visiting a local restroom two or three times during the workday for anonymous sexual encounters with other men.

In sex with his wife, Andrew was terrified of losing his

erection and had to keep homosexual fantasies in his head in order to reach orgasm. Despite himself, he invariably associated sexual release with solitary, narcissistic experiences: "Yeah, I keep my sexuality totally isolated in that act of focusing on my penis and the pornographic masturbation and I don't let it go anyplace," he told his therapist. "It's like a cannibalistic kind of feeling; it's like I want to ingest myself." And this narcissistic, pornographic sex life is something that is both deeply alienating but also deeply comfortable. Andrew, it seems, didn't "want to give up his relationship with his penis because if he did he would have to let in all of the pain he felt as a sixteen-year-old, the pain of witnessing his father beating his sister, his parents fighting, his peers bullying him in high school, his total aloneness, emptiness and shame about identifying with his mother." This feeling of void within was also the motive for his sexual encounters with other men: "Andrew spontaneously articulated how it really was highly likely that his wanting to incorporate the mass and bulk of men was a compensation for the feeling of emptiness he felt inside himself with regard to his own male identity as he was growing up."

We get the picture. This description of homosexuality links it both to a very early dysfunctional family relationship and then to a disordered, pathological sexuality. The twofold nature of this argument is critical, and it is worth reiterating. The origin of the homosexual's desire, the reparative therapists argue, requires that the disordered desire can *only* subsequently be met in a pathological fashion. Although Freud was careful to distinguish between an "invert" and a "pervert," the reparative therapists erase the difference. The homosexual's sexual needs, these therapists argue, are *by definition* unable to be satisfied by a sexual and emotional relationship with another man. They therefore comprise a pattern of self-destructive compulsion where the failure to find relief in sexual activity merely fuels the need for more such activity in a cycle that is as desperate as it is self-destructive.

All homosexual sexual behavior, both linked to narcissism and poor relations with the father, is therefore inherently neurotic: "The promiscuous sexuality of gays consisted of a series of one-night rituals designed to maintain distance from the tabooed father while bolstering their masculinity through contact with an externalized masculine ego-ideal and assuaging Oedipal guilt," writes Gerald Schoenewolf. "In these encounters they could each identify with the aggressor-father, and the sexuality was usually sadomasochistic and emotionally distant. Even homosexuals who had longer relationships had problematic sexual relations due to narcissistic interferences such as self-consciousness about their penises, bodies, etc."

Thus the self-defeating pattern is set. Socarides, as usual, puts it most bluntly: "In same-sex lovers, this sense of being alive [in sex] is very temporary. Their pleasure soon wears off and they end up . . . never finding a place where they can rest . . . They are forced into this pattern because, unlike heterosexuals, they do not possess any stable, gender-defined self-identity. They get a temporary sense of completeness from the sexual responses of their male partners. In a sense, this is a deficiency disease, which can only be remedied by expropriating the body and genitals of other males."

Thus the homosexual orientation is a pathology of a particularly crippling kind. It forbids by its very nature the expression of any sort of genuine love, it can never find any permanent satisfaction in homosexual contact, it is inherently compulsive, and it is ultimately a form of narcissism. Its only genuine expression is through same-sex sex, sex that objectifies and masks feelings of hatred, aggression, and control. Thus, "homosexuals have the central pathological mechanism common with anxiety neurotics, neurotic depressives, obsessive-compulsive neurotics," in the words of reparative therapist Richard Pullin. "The homosexual wish is an obsession like the perfectionistic compulsion of the obsessive-compulsive neurotic. Observe the nervous glances in a gay bar. They painfully examine every newcomer." It is this anxious, self-destructive psychopathology, present from an early age, that also leads, these therapists argue, to high levels of substance abuse and suicide.

I'VE PRESENTED THIS OUTLINE of the reparative theory of homosexuality at this length because it is important to see how it fits together as a whole. As an elaborate and total theory, it certainly cannot be dismissed as an improvised rationalization of bigotry, because its nuances are too refined and its observations too acute. I doubt whether any male homosexual will read these case studies without glimpsing something of himself in them, without identifying some shards of truth in their otherwise lurid accounts of extreme pain. The range of homosexual experience is truly vast, but it is still undeniable that certain patterns seem common, in particular an often deep and powerful bond with a mother, an estranged relationship with a father, and often dysfunctional sexual and emotional relationships. Like all generalizations, this is untrue in many particulars, and it can never be used to argue a particular outcome in any particular case. But anyone who has lived for long and kept his eyes and ears open, among male homosexuals, will recognize that some of these patterns are real, although their meaning is obviously open to interpretation greatly different from that of the reparative therapists. To say this is not, I think, a function of self-hatred. It is a function of honesty. And to deny it seems to me a stance that, in its defensiveness, concedes far too much to those who would pathologize homosexuals at their core.

And the argument of the reparative therapists is also useful because it represents in an articulate, explicit whole what many others are too embarrassed or too ashamed to say: that homosexuals are sick; that their conduct is inherently pathological; that homosexuality is not an orientation but a compulsive way of life; and that gay men, for reasons inherent to their nature, cannot be integrated into a healthy society. Certainly, it is no accident that such an argument is being revived at this time. Politically, the integration of homosexuals has reached such a point in our society that it seems only a matter of time before the anomalies of their different treatment—disparities in marriage law, military service, for example—

are overturned. The only hope for those who oppose this integration is to articulate again, however unpopular it may make them, the essential abnormality and disease that they believe homosexuality is.

But at each part of the argument, as Freud anticipated, there are many problems and some remarkable absences. They bear examination, if only because they may help sift the sometimes accurate observations the therapists have about homosexual men from their often far less plausible conclusions.

The first objection is the most far-reaching, if not the most persuasive. It is that the critical, early family pattern that the reparative therapists are outlining is not a cause of homosexuality, but a result of it. Under this rubric, the pattern of gay male development is cast in a radically different perspective. As a gay boy develops, his difference is intuited by his father and mother. The boy feels intuitively out of place with other heterosexual boys, withdraws, "feminizes" in response, and seeks a natural place of refuge with his mother. The father, more often than not, perceives this withdrawal as a rejection and reacts by further distancing the boy from his own interest and affection, thus further feminizing the child. In a subsequent defensive move, the mother protects her son more emphatically, thus perpetuating the vicious circle even further. The result is certainly for many gay children a traumatic and disturbing development, in which they endure considerable unhappiness and natural confusion about the nature of their gender identity. In other words, the reparative therapists are not misrepresenting what their patients are saying to them; they are simply misreading it. The "syndrome" emerges *from* the boy's nascent homosexuality, it doesn't cause it in the first place.

The psychoanalyst Richard Isay has presented one of the most accessible cases for this alternative scenario. Like the reparative therapists, he has noticed that a large majority of gay men recall a close bond with their mothers but, more noticeably, a difficult early relationship with their fathers. "Reports vary," Isay writes, "from 'my father was never around, he was too busy with his own job,' to 'he was victimized by my mother who was always the boss in the family,' to that of the abusive, unapproachable father." But unlike the reparative therapists, Isay believes that this is a *consequence* of the boys' homosexuality, not a cause of it. Thus, pre-homosexual boys, owing to a genetic same-sex predisposition, experience with their fathers something that pre-heterosexual boys experience with their mothers: an early Oedipal urge and overwhelming sexual attraction which they learn to repress and deny, just as pre-heterosexual boys do with their mothers. And this pattern may lead to a crisis in paternal relations, just as with straight boys it leads to a maternal crisis: "Fathers usually perceive such a child as being 'different' from other boys in the family, from themselves, or from their son's peers . . ."—"Why can't you be more *normal*?!"—". . . These boys may be more sensitive, have more aesthetic interests, may not be involved in competitive activities, and may be more seclusive than heterosexual boys . . . Some of the fathers of homosexual boys either consciously or unconsciously recognize that their sons have both a special need for closeness and an erotic attachment to them. These fathers may withdraw because of anxiety occasioned by their own homoerotic desires, which are usually unknown to them."

Part of the subtlety of this argument lies in the fact that it is not simply the fathers who engage in this distancing; it is the sons as well. Just as heterosexual boys naturally push away from their mothers at some point, homosexual boys also naturally push away from their fathers at the Oedipal stage. In fact, the distance may in some cases be more the responsibility of the child than of the bewildered and often wounded father. While loving, understanding mothers may respond to their heterosexual son's developmental separation by supporting it in part, and welcoming the son's emergence as a separate, male being, with the homosexual child, often no such support is available. Very few fathers will guide their young gay son into a stronger, homosexual identity in childhood and early adolescence. While the heterosexual child leaves the mother to bond with the father, and receives countless external affirmations of his budding masculinity, the gay child can meet ferocious social scorn among his peers for his reclusive, sometimes "sissy" persona and has nowhere to turn but his mother. He has, in other words, to endure the trauma of separating from the being he most longs for and loves (his father) without any compensating, socializing, affirming alternative. All he has is his mother, who will, more often than not, respond to the wounds her "sissy boy" child receives by protecting him all the more fiercely.

So the stories that gay men tell about themselves and their childhoods can sound remarkably similar and yet be subject to dramatically different interpretations. The stories of "Andrew" and "Nathan" can just as easily be fitted into Richard Isay's structure as their own therapist's. Andrew's overly close relationship with his mother, the comfort of her hairspray and cigarette smoke, contrasts with his deep woundedness at his father's rejection. But all of this can be just as plausibly explained as a *result* of Andrew's homosexuality, not as a cause of it.

There are also some aspects of Isay's theory that seem to explain some anomalies more neatly than the reparative therapists'. Take, for example, the fact that the distant father–overly close mother is obviously not sufficient in and of itself to cause homosexuality. If it were, then most of the generations born between 1930 and 1980 would be homosexual. There might also, perhaps, be a startling rise in homosexuality among African Americans in the last twenty years, when absent fathers have become the norm, rather than the exception. But, on the contrary, the incidence of homosexuality seems remarkably stable over time and place. The reparative therapists argue that such a typology is far too crude; that the issue is not broad family structures but unique family dynamics. What matters is not whether the father is there all the time but whether, when he is there, he forms a healthy emotional bond with his son. And besides, it is only in the most extreme cases of paternal rejection and maternal smothering that homosexuality results. But that begs a further question: What about siblings? Family dynamics can be remarkably similar for two brothers, and yet one can turn out gay, the other straight. The reparative therapists don't really have a watertight answer to this conundrum, except to argue again that interpersonal relationships are always unique, even within very close families and between two very similar siblings. But Isay has a much simpler alternative: only the gay child turns out gay! And the family pattern forms uniquely around that individual.

The two theories also take account of adult homosexual pathology, if in radically different ways. For the reparative therapists, as we've seen, the homosexual relationship is inherently pathological and can never result in a satisfying relationship. The only reason gay men seek out other men for emotional and sexual release, according to the reparative therapists, is to heal the wound created by their distant father. But, even in their desperate quest, they also know that the relationship cannot be the relationship they want it to be, because their lover is not their father, and they are not the woman their father desires. Hence the relationship crashes and burns as surely as it originally ignites. Gay men are trapped in a cycle that is driven first by their own sense of inadequacy as men, and second by the wounds they still carry from their childhood. The need to heal that wound is so great that, despite constant failure, they continue to plunge into homosexual contact after homosexual contact. Hence the high rate of homosexual promiscuity and short-term nature of most gay relationships.

But Isay can put a different twist on it. He can argue that the failure to sustain a long and successful relationship may indeed be related to the distant father, but that this is a function of a contingent and common form of emotional development that is ultimately driven by the family and society and not the homosexuality of the child himself. Indeed, the same patterns of dysfunction can be discerned in a heterosexual, if he is subjected to the same kind of distant fathering as a child. So therapy can help the homosexual relive some of those early traumas and wounds and so move beyond them into fulfilling relationships, in exactly the same way that therapy can help the heterosexual. Many straight men, after all, may come from dysfunctional family backgrounds and be unable to form long-term relationships as a result. Promiscuity and an inability to commit are not exclusively homosexual problems. It just so happens that the family's treatment of the pre-homosexual child may trigger the dysfunction more frequently and more prematurely than with many straights.

So Isay doesn't reject all the stereotypes. He merely normalizes them. Thus the smothering, narcissistic mother, so common in the accounts of the reparative therapists, reappears in Isay's account: "The sons of such mothers become men whose ambitions are so closely identified with those of their mothers and whose lives are so inseparable from them that they feel worthless except when pleasing them. These men tend to lack an emotional center of their own. They are usually enraged, feel enslaved to their mothers, and often develop masochistic tendencies because of their inability to tolerate this rage. As adults, they are constantly in search of their true selves and, consumed by this search, have difficulty forming lasting relationships." But the difference between Isay and the reparative therapists is simple: for Isay, this syndrome can just as easily occur among heterosexuals as among homosexuals. "Unlike most other psychoanalysts," he writes, "I have found no greater psychopathology in my gay patients than in my heterosexual patients."

THE TWO THEORETICAL STANCES, in many ways, are perfect mirrors of one another. And both, ironically, depend on a rejection of Freud's most fundamental premise: that all human beings are born omnisexual and therefore bisexual. For the reparative therapists, human beings are simply born heterosexual, and their biological gender mandates their future emotional and sexual roles. Or, in a fallback position, they argue that the resolution of the Oedipal complex so strongly propels us toward heterosexuality that we are better described by our proper destination than by where we begin. For Isay, some human beings are simply born homosexual, and this orientation determines their future emotional and sexual lives. For both sides, in other words, complex psychological arguments about homosexual and heterosexual development are underpinned by clear resorts to nature or to genes.

Take the reparative therapists first. For all their Freudianism, they also import into their arguments—because they have to import it—an argument about what is natural and what isn't. "The male-female design," Socarides baldly asserts, "is anatomically determined," a fact that mandates a social preference for heterosexuality. Elsewhere, he simply asserts the primacy of "normality," which is alternately natural—"the basic code and concept of life and biology," as exemplified in reproductive heterosexual intercourse—and social—inasmuch as "homosexuality cannot make a society or keep one going for very long." Socarides thus sees homosexuality as something likely to create gender conflict and to undermine successful child-rearing.

But surprisingly enough, Isay is dependent on a similar foundation. For Isay, and for other gay-friendly analysts, homosexuality is defensible simply because it is natural or "innate." He states at one point, "My clinical experience suggests that while the early environment has considerable influence on the manner in which sexuality is expressed, it has an indiscernible influence on the sex of the love object." Elsewhere he baldly describes it as "immutable from birth." He also refers to recent studies of twins which appear to suggest a strong genetic component to homosexuality. And you can see why he has to insist on this point. If he gives an inch on this ground—or even a month of neonatal life—then a much different and vastly more complicated dialogue would have to be engaged. Just as the reparative therapists have to rule out congenital bisexuality, or bring in an argument from biology or the design of nature to buttress their case, so Isay has to reach out to some external scientific arbiter to ground his account. Neither finds in Freud's delicate balance a stable place to conduct a discussion.

But Freud's delicate balance, however politically frustrating, is surely more convincing. The assertions of the reparative therapists about the self-evident design of nature are perhaps most easily dismissed. They bring to mind an old high school teacher of mine who would occasionally interrupt his Latin classes to digress on matters of high

moral import. One day, he famously defended masturbation to a group of (highly sympathetic) fifteen-year-old
boys because it was clear that men produced more semen
than they could possibly direct exclusively to procreation.
Single men did not naturally stop producing sperm, he
theorized, and, even when married, there were periods
(such as the wife's pregnancy) when it was impossible for
a man to have procreative, monogamous intercourse. So
what else was he supposed to do if not masturbate from
time to time? Anatomy was destiny. Nevertheless, on the
same grounds, he drew the line at homosexuality. It was,
as he simply put it, a matter of "the wrong hole." Some
orifices, it seems, were clearly designed by nature for certain functions; the anus was an out-hole, and the penis
clearly didn't belong there.

And to be perfectly honest, it would be churlish to deny
that this contains some intuitive common sense. In the
simple nature of their genitals, gay men do not differ
from straight men. Their semen contains sperm, they
have a natural capacity to procreate, and their genitals
are clearly capable of reproduction. If you place any cre-
dence on the notion of what nature seems to have
designed, the discrepancy between this and the sexual
orientation of gay men is a difficult thing to dismiss. I
remember when I was growing up, it occurred to me that
my "difference" should surely at some point be reflected
in my anatomy. One of the reasons I was nervous during
puberty was that part of me thought it would reveal that I
was not like other boys; that certain things would not
happen to me; that my voice would not break, my body

would not grow, my genitals would not develop. I had a nightmare once of looking down to my crotch and seeing nothing there.

But of course, the salience of this discrepancy is one that would impress itself most vividly on a thirteen-year-old. As we grow up, we realize that there are many instances when anatomy is not always and everywhere destiny. Our mouths, for example, are clearly "designed" to ingest food, and yet they are also the way we kiss. Is one function somehow more natural than the other? We also use our mouths to smile. Is this an illicit use for them or a more elevated one? A perversion or an intrinsically human deployment of our bodies? Our genitals are surely subject to the same dilemmas. For men and women, urination and orgasm are somehow connected to very proximate physical sites. Is this a joke—or a symbol? And if nature itself has indicated that our bodies can be understood to have a variety of meanings and functions, then why should loving sexual relations between two people of the same sex be excluded from permissibility?

Taken in its crudest, functional sense, for example, nature would seem to forbid any intercourse during pregnancy or during menstruation; it would forbid it after menopause; it would forbid celibacy, contraception, and fellatio; and, for young men, in particular, it would seem to forbid monogamy. Yet we rightly subject these apparently "natural" injunctions to the judgment of a larger human, social, or moral compass. Of course, it might be possible to create a theory of man's natural ends which takes account of biology but supplements it with a more comprehensive picture of moral goods (that, after all, is the project we have come to call "natural law"). And it might be possible to construct such an argument in a way that would discourage certain behaviors and encourage others, and endorse loving gay relationships in the same way that we might endorse loving infertile relationships (or not, as the case may be). But the reparative therapists do not engage this discussion and seem remarkably deaf to its subtleties. They are content merely to assert homosexual abnormality and, when challenged about the possible origins of that pathology, to invoke the crude imperatives of the "wrong hole" or of "male-female design" and the "basic code and concept of life and biology."

Those latter imperatives are particularly fraught. In what way, for example, does the existence of homosexuality deny something called the "male-female design"? Homosexuality exists among both men and women, and neither gay men nor lesbians seek to eradicate or deny the existence of the other. It certainly doesn't imply the abolition of heterosexuality—far from it. Indeed, without such a design, homosexuals, just as much as heterosexuals, would cease to exist. Nor does the resilience of homosexuality threaten to eclipse or unbalance male-female symmetry in human relations. It merely reflects that symmetry—in its bifurcation into lesbianism and male homosexuality—in another way. And because it has always been, and always will be, a small fraction of any society, it is far more likely to be influenced disproportionately by the majority than the other way round.

As to the "basic code and concept of life and biology," it is hard to know what that might mean. Taken to its logical conclusion, the basic code of life and biology is most readily interpreted as the survival of the fittest. But if we are to take our moral direction from such purely biological signposts, then it is not only homosexuals who are undesirable. So are the infertile and the unproductive, the old and the infirm, the monogamous and the disabled. Indeed, anyone who chooses not to procreate— priests, single women, childless couples—could be seen as violating the basic code. It is a chilling thought.

But in some respects, Isay's appeals to nature, though far less crude than the reparative therapists', are almost as unpersuasive. What could it possibly mean, for example, to assert that a child is immutably homosexual at birth? Freud's notion that the newborn baby is omnisexual is difficult enough to accept, but that its sexuality is already oriented toward members of its own sex at the age of six months stretches credulity to the breaking point. And if the genetic component is merely a predictor of an eventual homosexual orientation, then in what does that genetic component consist?

Isay points to the recent evidence of genetic similarities between homosexual men. In one study of 115 gay men, for example, identical twins were twice as likely to share a homosexual orientation as fraternal twins. And a recent study of forty families in which there were two gay brothers showed a remarkably high incidence of a particular genetic sequence on the X chromosome. But, as even the scientists conducting the inquiries insist, these studies are a far cry from the notion of a "gay gene" and beg as many questions as they resolve. In a species like *Homo sapiens*, where a disproportionately vast amount of child development takes place outside the womb, especially in the first three years of life, the whole distinction between genetic and environmental influences is suspect in the first place. Indeed, it is a distinctively human trait—and a key to the species' survival—that environment plays a disproportionate part in human development. As some evolutionary psychologists have pointed out, the brain of a human newborn, for example, is one quarter the size of an adult's, compared with two-thirds the size in a monkey. It is particularly adaptive to its early environment, and influenced by it. To say that an identity and behavior as complex, as varied, and as deep as homosexual orientation, are somehow present in that newborn (or even unborn) brain is particularly suspect. It would be bizarre, to be sure, if some sort of genetic imprint were not at work in the development of homosexuality. But it would also be bizarre if environmental influences did not play a profound role as well. No responsible scientist would argue—or has argued—otherwise.

So Isay's simple assertion of innate homosexuality is as unappealing as Socarides's assertion of the biological injunction to anathematize it. The most reasonable inference from the genetic studies returns us, in fact, to Freud, or at least to some version of him. Perhaps the best we can infer is that some correlation of (as yet unknown) genetic factors may *predispose* a child to homosexuality, but those factors alone are probably not sufficient to bring it about. In other words, like most forms of human behavior, it's almost certainly a little bit of both, and both sides in the debate would be a great deal more convincing if they conceded the point. Indeed, it is yet another depressing consequence of the emotional polarization of this debate that this obvious starting point is one we have taken pains to avoid.

How exactly this combination of genetic predisposition interacts with environment is what Freud attempted incompletely to unravel. And it's not surprising he failed. The mind, indeed, reels at the possibilities. The environmental incentives could vary from individual to individual as often as family dynamics vary, affecting in turn both the degree and the nature of the child's homosexual orientation. And the nature of what genetically predisposes a child to homosexuality could also conceivably vary. One scenario, for example—one that fits both some behavioral studies, and much of the clinical evidence of the psychoanalysts (reparative and otherwise)—emphasizes the child's genetic predisposition toward a sex-neutral characteristic such as aggression or physical activity. It's a good example of what a calmer inquiry into the origins of homosexuality might reveal.

The theory, developed most originally by the psychologist Daryl Bem, posits a mix of factors. Bem suggests that a boy who is genetically predisposed to be more passive, reflective, and sensitive than others may, in certain circumstances, be constitutionally predisposed to homosexuality. The orientation begins to take shape in the boy's response to early peer interaction. Being more timid and less active than his peers, the pre-homosexual boy may withdraw from gender-bonding communal activities like team sports. In that process, he becomes estranged from his own gender and, in a common psychological pattern, comes to eroticize what is alien to him. Thus, in Bem's words, the "exotic" becomes "erotic." Bem completely re-jects the traditional psychoanalytic family model, but in some ways, you can see how the two theories are compati-ble. It is, after all, the child's "passive" estrangement from his father, according to the reparative therapists, that causes him later to eroticize the father's masculinity. So here are two independent homosexual-development mod-els to start with: the sports-team model and the father-son model. And we may well see gay men who have a combination of the two or a range of other as yet un-known predispositions that, given a range of family or peer dynamics, might engender wholly different routes to same-sex orientation.

BUT IF WE ACCEPT some version of this homosexual tra-jectory (and it seems to me the most plausible), we still have to resolve the reparative therapists' essential point, which is that, whatever the genetic predisposition and however complex the environmental model attached to it, the result is still always and everywhere a form of sex-ual pathology. And without resorting to Isay's unconvinc-ingly crude notion of innate homosexuality, it's not too hard to see why this may not necessarily be the case.

The first, and most obvious, problem is that the evi-dence for inherent pathology is largely drawn from the clients of the reparative therapists themselves. And their clients are, by their very nature, likely to be more dis-turbed, conflicted, and pained by their orientation than many others—and therefore more prone to pathological behavior that temporarily eases their psychic pain. They are not merely so conflicted as to seek therapy; they are so conflicted as to seek therapy from people who have publicly committed themselves to curing individuals of what they call a homosexual affliction. Once again, Freud beats us to the punch. As he wryly remarked, "Perverts who can obtain satisfaction rarely have occasion to come in search of analysis." It would surely be somewhat dangerous to extrapolate theories about the general population from such an anguished and conflict-ridden couch.

But assume, for a moment, that the reparative therapists are exaggerating but not inventing, that they are correct in seeing somewhat higher levels of sexual pathology among gay men than among straight men: more promiscuity; more sexual objectification; fewer meaningful relationships; more repetitive, anonymous sexual compulsion. Are there factors outside the intrinsic nature of homosexuality that could explain these? Does it follow that these behaviors are necessarily a result of the very nature of the homosexual condition? Is there indeed any logical link at all between the way a sexual orientation emerges and the way it subsequently expresses itself?

Perhaps the best indicator of where the answer to these questions may be found lies in the areas where the reparative therapists are uncharacteristically silent. And these silences converge on two clear areas: the role of social and familial hostility in undermining gay children's self-esteem, and therefore their emotional and psychological functioning, and the reparative therapists' almost total lack of interest in the emotional and sexual development of lesbian girls and women.

*

THE REASON the reparative therapists don't want to raise the possibility of social hostility being primarily responsible for higher levels of gay male psychopathology is obvious. It would suggest to their patients that the best way to combat their own distress is to work for political and social change, rather than to search within for a psychoanalytic cure. But it is surely obvious—even to those who want to "cure" homosexuals—that any gay child must endure social and psychological pressures that are as acute as they are isolating. For reasons such children do not understand and cannot control, they feel different from others at a time when the pressure to be the same is at its developmental peak. This difference is often stigmatized and entrenched by the brutality of childhood life. There is no epithet more designed to wound a young boy than "faggot" or "sissy." And the insults may come most insistently from those toward whom the young homosexual is most attracted. There is often no refuge from this, except to an internal world of imagination or longing, a place where he can dream of acceptance, or perhaps vindication against his wounding friends and enemies. This is why, I suspect, so many intelligent gay boys harbor grandiose ambitions, or display precocious scholarship, or narcissistic impulses. They are driven inward not by any intrinsic nature, but as a form of protection against the taunts and weapons of the people around them.

And of course, in our gender-polarized world, they are beset by a crisis of identity. Am I a boy or a girl? Some respond to this by actually adopting the mannerisms or affect of girls, in some crude attempt to make sense of themselves. Others may overcompensate by doing the opposite, donning the mantle of hypermasculinity, competing in sports more aggressively than others, forcing their true selves even deeper into hiding, selves which they may not retrieve until much later in life, or never. The isolation breeds both a driving need to rebel and a desperate need to be accepted, and the gay child may grow up oscillating violently between the two.

And his relationships may therefore fall into this pattern as well. He both longs for other boys and men and yet associates them with rejection and pain. So in later life he seeks unconsciously to replay this pattern by seeking out men who he knows will reject or hurt him. Or his sexuality, formed first in secret and for so long forbidden a natural pattern of interaction with other boys, gets separated in his mind from friendship or companionship, and so tends to be expressed in compulsive, anonymous, or narcissistic adventures, adventures that may relieve his loneliness temporarily but serve later merely to reinforce his sense of deepening isolation. Or he understands from his family and friends that his sexuality is something inherently shameful, that it deserves punishment, and so he finds himself in later life pursuing sex that is inherently sadomasochistic or love that will never be reciprocated. In this way, he can both express his anger at the sexual objects who once tormented him, or submit to them in a replay of his deep sense of unworthiness.

The reparative therapists are right, it seems to me, about much of this. This is often pathological behavior, if by pathological we mean repetitive, desperate, and conflict-ridden behavior that must always fail to solve the problem that occasions it. Such behavior can be found in many places in the gay male world—perhaps more often than in the straight world. But the reparative therapists are surely rash in the simple conclusions they draw from it. Such behavior may not be so much a consequence of homosexuality, as they claim, but a consequence of growing up homosexual in a world that seeks to deny your very existence.

My mother remembers an incident I have subsequently forgotten. When I was only eight, I came to her and asked if God really knew everything about you, if He could see into every part of you and know exactly what you were thinking and feeling. Yes, she replied. "Then there's no hope for me, Mum," I apparently said, and walked back into my bedroom, despondent. For much of my adolescence, this despondency intensified. I became withdrawn at home, brittle, neurotic; as I entered puberty, the panic mounted. I found myself, in an attempt to impose some order on a chaotic internal existence, washing my hands and feet compulsively, carefully avoiding cracks in the sidewalk, compulsively vacuuming the house, cleaning the kitchen, tidying my room. At high school, some kind of escape from young heterosexual bonding loomed in the form of academic work, and so I plowed all my attentions into Latin grammar and English composition. At the weekends, alarmed at the possibility that I might have to interact with girls as a sexual being, I devoted myself to my homework, appeasing my anxiety by perfecting every nook and cranny of my academic requirements.

For some sort of relief, I took part in school plays, acting out roles that I couldn't play in real life, and became a star debater, grandiosely fantasizing about a future life as prime minister or war leader. And as my internal imagination flourished, my emotional life went into a kind of neurotic vacuum. I grew further and further apart from my father, consumed with an anger and hatred that terrified me, and closer and closer to my mother, with a mixture of desperate need and incipient resentment. My only form of bearable relationship was with friends, intellectual soulmates, people in whom I intuited some kind of unspoken bond (many of whom turned out to be gay). Love was out of the question, sex a powerful and uncontrollable urge that I associated increasingly with images of the men I knew I could never have, men like my father, and men unlike my father, men whose only response to hearing that I desired them would be to beat me to a pulp. For years, because I could not conceive of an actual relationship in which to express my sexuality, I lived sexually and emotionally in a world of fantasy, masturbation, and self-contained shame. I learned to kill off sexual yearnings for the boys I cared about and fell for, and to reattach sexual attraction to boys who would never know and never guess. Is it any wonder that, having learned my sexuality this way, it became hard later to attach it to meaningful or deeply intimate relationships? Or that it took years of effort to reimagine my sexual being as something worthy of love rather than objectification or hate?

When I hear stories of gay teenage suicides, or that 40 percent of runaways are gay, or that gay teens suffer high rates of depression or drug abuse or alcoholism, I do not need much of an explanation. I remember, and shudder. Not that every young gay life is as bleak as this. Plenty of young boys experience a far milder form of alienation. Some have no family trauma that they can recall, and remember only a slight discrepancy between themselves and other boys. Others still (myself included) may not have fit into the category of being estranged from their own gender at all times. I was lucky enough to come from a culture where male-male interaction was not exclusively organized around team sports or dating girls. As a child, I enjoyed playing with other boys, rambling through the countryside in gangs, cycling together, interacting in a completely natural way. From the age of ten onward, I had virtually no female friends. My high school was composed entirely of boys, and I felt extremely at ease there. As a specially gifted geek and prizewinning debater, I had a male status of my own and felt no particular insecurity about my masculinity. No part of me ever wanted to be a girl or, at least consciously, to gain masculinity by somehow absorbing the maleness of others.

But each homosexual path is unique. Unpicking its causes and consequences can take a lifetime of introspection. When I look at my friends and acquaintances over the years I see a whole range of types: men who primarily long for lost, masculine peers; men who just missed getting on the baseball team and still yearn for the bonding they can never regain; men whose extreme closeness to their fathers made them feel paradoxically more emotionally distant, because of their secret homosexuality; men whose mothers dominated their existence (and still do) to the point that they can have no form of emotional relationship at all; men who were on every school team, excelled in every sport, and long for the aesthetic geek figure that they really felt they were; men who have never given a moment's thought to why they're attracted to men and find relationships natural and easy; gay men who marry women for the sake of their mothers and who appease their anxieties by manic careerism; effeminate men who vent their anxieties by dominating others in sex or who compensate for their insecurities by constructing vast, muscular torsos to intimidate and threaten their heterosexual peers; masculine jocks whose primary attraction is to effeminate queens; men who seem to be asexual and who settle easily into monogamous long-term relationships; men who never progress from cruising adult bookstores; men from traditional backgrounds who told their parents when they were thirteen; and sons of liberal shrinks who face a lifetime of explanation. I mention this range simply because it is a reminder that all human types are foiled by human reality. Switch genders in it, and I'm sure you'll recognize a whole range of heterosexual pathologies as well. Pathology is never universal, and rarely complete, even in one human being. And the possible theoretical paths to homosexuality that have been advanced do little to explain the stunning variety of human experience, homo or hetero. For every rule, there is an exception; for every incidence of sickness, there is a startling display of mental health.

And it is too easy to relate pathology to homosexuality by simple tautology. Because many of us have absorbed from the culture that something about homosexuality is wrong, we often indiscriminately ascribe aberrant behavior among homosexuals to their homosexuality and not to something else. Take the contrast between two recent crime-story figures: O. J. Simpson and Andrew Cunanan. Both were clearly prone to pathological behavior. But, in everyday parlance, Cunanan was a gay killer; but Simpson was not spoken of as a straight killer. Cunanan was described as someone who led a pathological homosexual lifestyle, full of sex and drugs, prostitution, promiscuity, and even, it was alleged, sadomasochism. Although commentators rarely made an explicit connection between his psychopathic tendencies and his homosexuality, the very context in which he was discussed made the connection clear.

Compare it to the story of O. J. Simpson. Simpson's story was never played as a case study in heterosexual pathology. But, in many ways, it was a classic of the genre. Simpson engaged in every pathological heterosexual male behavior imaginable: he was highly promiscuous and acutely jealous; he was a part of an all-male professional sports culture that celebrated promiscuity; he was compulsively violent and sadistic toward his wife. Yet, insofar as Simpson was regarded as symptomatic of anything, it was his race that was mentioned—despite the fact that he was far less typical of African Americans in general than he was of many pathological heterosexual men.

The point I'm trying to make here is that pathology can be an extremely slippery thing. We can see it where it doesn't truly exist, and we can be blind to it when it stares us in the face. And we often assign it to reasons that are already planted in our minds, rather than to anything real in the evidence. We are particularly prone to discern it in minorities that are defined by the majority, people whose very terms of discourse have been created by the people attempting to keep them in their place. This is not say that pathologies do not really exist among, say, gay men or African Americans. It is to say that they exist elsewhere as well, and we would do well to check ourselves before we too easily assert them as intrinsically related to something that also defines an individual's cultural or emotional identity.

Nevertheless, it is also true that, even in the healthiest and least traumatized homosexual life, certain conflicts emerge which have a root in the inherent nature of homosexuality itself. Just because the reparative therapists crudely associate every gay male problem with homosexuality doesn't mean that all gay problems are really other sorts of problems or a result of social isolation. To name a simple one: many heterosexual marriages are kept together, deepened, and strengthened by the addition of children. Although many gay couples, especially lesbians, do have children, it is still true that many more gay couples than straight couples are childless, and therefore without this rampart of support. It seems to me quite ridiculous to deny this difference or to ignore how, in this instance, a gay relationship may actually take greater resources of intimacy and risk and engagement to survive in the long term.

But just as certainly, childlessness is a contingent (and not inevitable) quality of many gay relationships. It is hard to infer from it that such relationships are always less stable than heterosexual ones, or somehow intrinsically so. What of successful childless heterosexual relationships?

Failed gay marriages with children? The range of human experience is too vast for such a generalization. But other intrinsic characteristics of the homosexual relationship, characteristics the reparative therapists are keen to point out, are less easily put to one side.

And one of those characteristics surely stems from the fact that every gay relationship brings two men or two women together. In such a relationship, unlike the heterosexual one, there are some inherent issues of narcissism and gender similarity that cannot be casually dismissed. Take a primary and fascinating dilemma, to which the reparative therapists constantly and enthusiastically return: if some sort of longing for lost masculinity is central to male homosexual desire (just as a longing for lost femininity is central to male heterosexual desire), then how can true gender complementarity happen in a gay relationship? How can both sides feel fully complete? Among heterosexuals, the answer is superficially easy: the heterosexual male finds his lost femininity in the female, and the heterosexual female finds her lost masculinity in the male. There is some sort of balance possible here. But among two men or two women, there is a missing correlation, an absence of complementarity, a discrepancy which must, the reparative therapists argue, lead to an intrinsically unstable relationship.

The argument would go something like this. Start with a stereotype, which, like most stereotypes, is partly documented in reality. It is of a bonding between an aggressive, masculine man and a passive, feminine man, simulating the heterosexual relationship—but without two genders present. Scan the classified section of a gay paper, and you will see this typology reflected in a sizable proportion of the personal ads seeking merely sex. "Tops" seek "bottoms"; "butches" seek "femmes." For the reparative therapists, this simulacrum of the heterosexual order is yet another sign of the inherent contradictions of male homosexual desire and its inherently "deceptive" quality. For in such a relationship, it is impossible for both sides to reach completeness. If homosexuality is an attempt to find the lost masculine within by incorporating it in the sexual act, then only one-half of the equation works. Only the passive partner encounters a true, penetrative male, and even then, he is reminded that his partner is not a true male, not someone who is actually attracted to women. As for the active participant, his interaction with a submissive feminine partner hardly satisfies his need for an infusion of masculinity; he can merely simulate some vicarious masculinity by playacting the dominant hetero male.

For each, therefore, the interaction is doomed to be dissatisfying. The bottoms might momentarily appease their longing for the masculine, but only by becoming feminized and therefore intensifying their own internal gender conflict. The tops, on the other hand, not only fail to repair their own masculine deficiency by assuming the role of the masculine but, because their partner is male, also understand, in some deep part of themselves, that they are not fully male because they are not making love to a woman. And so their conflict intensifies as well. The sexual act, while temporarily alleviating both men's distress, in the long run only serves to accentuate it, making it even more necessary to seek further means of relieving the psychological pressure. Which leads to more sex, which tightens the vise even further.

Not so long ago, gay culture more completely fit into this archetype. As the historian George Chauncey has detailed, homosexuals were once categorized into two complementary groups: "normal" men and "fairies." Normal men, more often than not, married women but sought homosexual outlets by being fellated from time to time by feminine, passive fairies. Fairies, more often than not, lived on the margins of society, breaking up their isolation by occasional, often anonymous contact in submissive and humiliating roles with normal men. The roles were rigid and distinct, rarely to be confused, and clearly, in varying degrees, pathological. In many cases, no real relationships were formed, sex was silent and functional, conducted in dark and often public places; fantasies and role-playing determined a large part of the interaction. Some were able to vent their homosexual desire without disturbing their self-identity as heterosexuals and men; the others were able to manage their gender conflicts by simply taking the form of women in sex and behaving in other areas of their life as a third sex altogether.

It is easy to see how this conflicted, painful way of life fits into the reparative therapists' pattern. But it begs an obvious question: How is it that, in recent times, these paradigms have sharply declined among gay men to such a point that, for a large plurality, they scarcely exist? If such a pattern is inherent to the genesis of the homosexual condition, then how can it be so culturally flexible? In the 1970s and early 1980s, when homosexuality gained more freedom of expression, these categories did not intensify, as the reparative therapists might have expected. On the contrary, they swiftly declined, allowing for a far wider degree of sexual and emotional expression.

The proof of this change, tragically enough, can be found in the spread of HIV. Indeed, the spread of the virus, which is primarily transmitted by anal sex, would have been stopped in its tracks if the bifurcation of gay men into "tops" and "bottoms" had remained rigid, because there would have been no way for the virus to be passed along beyond one, single encounter. What was happening—and is still happening—is that, in the sexual act, the whole notions of masculinity and femininity were becoming slowly estranged from the notions of "active" and "passive." As homosexual men became more integrated human beings, as the closet collapsed, as anonymous public sex became supplemented by relationships between two mature adults, the notion of such heterosexually conceived role playing declined.

To be sure, in the recesses of the sexual imagination, in the moments when sexual release took over from any form of interpersonal relationship, or love, or commitment, such tropes endured. And they endure still, in the culture of the sexual classifieds, in those cultures—especially African American and Latino—where the closet (and hostility to homosexuals) is far more entrenched, and particularly among men with the most severe internal conflicts about their sexual orientation. But elsewhere, sexual roles have become much more fluid as homosexuality has become more accepted, and as masculinity has ceased to be understood as somehow contradictory to homosexuality but as compatible with it.

This development suggests again that the allegedly self-contradictory need for the masculine-as-heterosexual may not be intrinsic to homosexual desire or love at all; it may merely be intrinsic to *arrested* homosexual desire, desire that is still plagued by emotional or gender insecurities, desire that is still in profound conflict with the person's full sense of self. That, of course, may be why the reparative therapists saw so much of it: because their patients are among the most conflicted and arrested homosexuals in the population.

So another scenario beckons. It is one in which homosexuality may indeed be rooted in some early psychological yearning for the father figure or the estranged, masculine peer but in which the tensions this may create can be abated considerably by self-esteem, by the experience of love, and by a deeper and more secure sense of one's own homosexual masculinity. In this way, homosexuality is not so different from its heterosexual counterpart. There too, the origin of the orientation may be a displaced longing for the mother figure or the estranged female peer, but its adult expression need not be limited by this displacement. The man may learn not to seek his mother in every woman he loves, and he may see in sex and love less a rote expression of rigid gender roles than an invitation to engage in a sexual and emotional dialogue with another being, someone whose gender is the beginning of the attraction but far from the end of it.

The homosexual relationship will still differ, I think, by not encountering a radically different gender in love and sexuality, just as it will differ by not including an intrinsic ability to create new life within that relationship. And it would be foolish to deny such obvious (and, in one sense, limiting) differences. But that is different from saying that a homosexual relationship cannot inherently work; that inherited notions of constrictive gender roles and an intrinsic sense of gender inadequacy will always doom a gay relationship; that gay love must somehow always see itself as a lesser form—and an often gross parody—of the heterosexual relationship. Whenever two human beings enter into a self-risking relationship, they start a conversation the course of which is never predetermined. Human beings are more than their genders and the roles their genders have assumed. And part of the mystery and promise of love—especially in a liberal society—is that it is a place where individuals are free to explore the limits of nature and the limits of trust in ways no outsider can ever understand or truly know. So a gay relationship may choose to conform to a rigid separation of gender roles, or it may develop in such a way that no such roles exist, or it may evolve so that such roles are shared or exchanged or played with in a constant, improvised dialogue of trust and daring. That adventure—its risks, its opportunities, and its potential—is just as deep and as exhilarating for a gay couple as it is for a straight one.

There may even be some advantages in a gay relationship. While the presence of two people of the same gender in a love affair may contain the danger of narcissism, the flip side may be a capacity for greater mutual understanding. Men and women, as we are so often reminded, constantly have to confront the pitfalls of miscommunication, of misunderstanding, of radically different priorities and moods and physical needs and ways of thinking.

Some of this is socially induced; some is clearly driven by different biological impulses and drives. In order to reach a level of intimacy, a man and a woman have first to cross this difficult and treacherous river of difference. Gay couples are spared such a journey. They begin not only with a mutual understanding of their own gender but also with a shared knowledge of their own often similar struggle to come to terms with their difference. At last, such a difference may bring two people together rather than push them further apart. It is a bond, like a shared ethnicity or religion or background, that can make a love deeper and longer lasting.

And precisely because such a same-sex relationship cannot in itself create new life, it is more pellucidly entered into for its own sake. It is not and never can be for the sake of children, and its meaning can never be reduced to something it produces rather than something it simply is. It is for this reason, of course, that some ancient and Renaissance writers disparaged heterosexual marriage—because it was so clearly biologically useful, and its usefulness somehow detracted from its purity. If love is its own justification and its own reward, then offspring can be understood as a superfluity, and even a drawback.

Of course, such a secure same-sex relationship requires a firm self-confidence in one's own gender. For those boys and girls who have internalized their orientation as a masculine or feminine deficiency, it will take work and time and effort as adults to strengthen that self-confidence and to undo the damage that was once so brutally done. If our society evolves into a greater acceptance of gay men and women, if the subject becomes more discussible, then the damage to children's self-esteem may not be so great, and the pathologies may not be so widespread. But the syndrome of damage will never, I think, be fully erased. It will never be easy, even in the most tolerant of homes and neighborhoods, to be a gay child. And those early wounds make homosexuality, alas, inevitably more prone to adult dysfunction and pathology. It means that insecure gay adults will always cling, to a greater or lesser extent, to the protections of gender mannerisms, of excessive masculinity or caricatured femininity, of "top" and "bottom" and "femme" and "butch," to mask and obscure the pain they once felt and to ironize or mock the structures that once nearly obliterated them.

It means also that narcissism and promiscuity will likely endure as intermittent elements of gay culture, just as camp and drag will. But we will measure our progress by the extent to which these ways of managing the pain recede, by the extent to which we successfully reclaim our gender from the people who would deny it to us, including ourselves. The future for gay men and women is one in which our gender, male or female, is neither abolished nor caricatured, but reclaimed. It is one in which being a man will always and everywhere be different from being a woman but will be compatible in every respect with loving another man, just as being a woman will always and everywhere be different from being a man but will be compatible in every respect with loving another woman.

I will be accused in this scenario of both intolerance and gender radicalism. It will seem as if, perhaps, I am stigmatizing (or condescending to) those who parody the masculine or feminine: the leather daddies and lipstick lesbians, the drag queens and diesel dykes, the purveyors and marketers of camp and irony. But nothing could be further from the truth. These extraordinary products of a long history of isolation and marginalization are marvels of revolt, of invention, and, often, of beauty. Insofar as they are inventive products of a culture of energetic difference, symbols of a determination to survive against considerable odds, they merit an intense admiration and defense. But insofar as these cultural expressions are also products of deep and searing anxiety, of the inability to be a publicly gay man or woman except as a caricature of one gender or another, then they are no more to be clung to than excruciating racial stereotypes. There is a difference between a culture of difference and a rationalization of pain. And clinging to the manifestations of isolation is no substitute for abolishing the isolation itself.

I will also be accused also, from the other side of the political tracks, of wanting to do away with gender altogether, of ignoring the profound biological differences between men and women, of seeking to erase the psychological distinction between male and female. But there is a difference between saying that sexual orientation should not be linked to inverted notions of masculinity or femininity and saying that the genders have no profound biological and psychological differences. Or that the vast journey between a heterosexual man and woman is not a wondrous, worthwhile, and ennobling one. My own view is that those gender differences, if anything, are deeper than the differences between heterosexuals and homosexuals. Which is to say that lesbian culture is always likely to

be far more estranged from gay male culture than heterosexual culture, and vice versa.

WHICH IS WHERE the reparative therapists' second, and
most glaring, lacuna presents itself, a lacuna I mentioned.
Why the extraordinary absence of lesbian women in their
studies and papers? Why, in the careful analysis of how
homosexual orientation is inherently pathological in its
genesis and development, are lesbians so starkly ignored?
One answer, of course, is simply historical, if hardly persuasive: women have simply long been ignored by male
doctors and psychoanalysts. Why should the reparative
therapists be any different? But the question acquires
more urgency when you think more precisely about what
it is that these therapists describe as homosexual pathology. In their view, it is an intractable gender-deficiency
disease, compulsively medicated by temporary sexual
gratification and the correspondingly high levels of
promiscuity, depression, dysfunction, and addiction this
brings in its wake. So why ignore lesbians in this context?

It cannot be because lesbian orientation is rooted in a
radically different early-childhood pattern. As we've seen,
Freud saw male and female homosexualities as rooted
in very similar patterns of maternal closeness and paternal distance. So could it have anything to do with the
fact that the glaring absence of male homosexual pathologies among lesbians suggests a different conclusion
about male homosexuality? That what is really at issue is
not the intrinsically pathological nature of same-sex

orientation, or even simply the social stigma attached to homosexuality, but the stark and predictable patterns of behavior in a sexual and emotional universe comprised entirely of *men*?

Whether this universe is a cultural or biological construct is irrelevant for the sake of this argument. Culturally, men are brought up in our society to see sex as a form of conquest, to view sexual experience as something to enjoy and be proud of, and to see monogamy and fidelity as unwelcome, if necessary, infringements on their sexual expression. They are therefore often more disposed to be promiscuous and sexually pathological in their behavior than women. In response to this enculturation, our society has established solid if often ineffective social norms to restrain male sexual irresponsibility—the most powerful and central of which is marriage. Except, of course, for homosexual men, for whom no social restraints of this kind are deemed necessary or even desirable, and among whom promiscuity is subject to far more social criticism than among their heterosexual peers.

In terms of the relatively new field of evolutionary psychology, there are also powerful arguments that would predict a culture of sexual license in a universe of men, whatever the cultural context surrounding it. These arguments, taken to their logical conclusion, suggest at least a plausible alternative explanation for the reparative therapists' account of intrinsic homosexual pathology.

A very crude summary of the evolutionary psychology case might go something like this: it is in the evolutionary interest of the human species as whole to see the widest level of genetic variation in its next generation (to protect against disease and environmental hazards). It is similarly in the interest of every human being to see that his or her own genes are passed on as widely (i.e., as promiscuously) as possible. But it is also in the interest of the species for its offspring, which require a long pregnancy and a longer period of intensive nurturing, to have attentive parents and stable family environments. Both men and women are therefore conflicted in evolutionary terms between promiscuity and monogamy—both being necessary for the successful propagation of the species.

But—and here is the rub—the balance of interests for each sex is slightly different. Men produce sperm constantly. Although they want their offspring successfully reared, their main purpose in securing a wide range of genetic outlets is defined by a) their ability to attract women, b) the small amount of time it takes for them to impregnate the woman, and c) the number of women they can inseminate. For women, however, the equation is skewed by the fact that it is she who has to spend nine months carrying the child (during which time she cannot have another child) and possibly several years nurturing it. So, although she too wants to spread her genes as widely as possible, she tends to be more picky in her choice of sexual partner than the male. She wants a mate who will be responsible and hang around after the night of passion, since she will be the one left literally holding the baby if he wanders off.

The science writer Deborah Blum vividly illustrates this imbalance by pointing to the *Guinness Book of World Records*. The male world record for offspring, she points out, is held by an ancient Mongolian warlord who sired some 888 children; the female world record belongs to an eighteenth-century Russian woman who allegedly gave birth to 69 (she had a lot of triplets). The disparity between those two statistics tells you something about not simply male power but its biological dimensions: men can achieve their evolutionary purpose far less responsibly than women. Or look at it another way. Blum cites a statistic that says the average length of heterosexual, penetrative copulation in America is four minutes. But the normal length of a pregnancy is nine months. In those two numbers you see a crude, evolutionary disparity in investment which men and women have in their offspring. Whichever way you look at it, from a simple, evolutionary perspective, men have more invested in the quantity of their sexual partners, and women more in the quality.

This would lead, the evolutionary psychologists argue, to certain plausible observations about male and female culture. Men tend to be more geared sexually to their partner's physical appearance, to instant sexual gratification, and to a larger number of partners; women tend to be attracted more by their partner's personality, to the erotic context of a relationship, and to a single man. Of course, this varies greatly among individuals; and there are plenty of monogamously inclined men and sexually adventurous women. But as a general rule, it conforms to our experience. How else to explain, for example, the avalanche of pornography directed at men, and the cascade of soap operas and romantic novels aimed at women? Evolutionary psychologists also point to testosterone comparisons

to see underlying gender imbalance in levels of promiscuity. Blum cites a study that shows that in monogamous
bird species, females tend to have the same testosterone
levels as males; among humans, men have ten times the
female level. This is not to say that somehow women, in
general, are less sexual than men; merely that their sexuality is of a different kind—less instant, less aggressive,
less restless, and more humane.

But whatever the origins of this disparity (and for the
purposes of this argument, it hardly matters whether
they are found in culture or evolution), it is hard to deny
that men and women in our society are, in general, very
different in terms of their attitude toward sex and love.
Now what might this tell us about the pathologies of gay
male culture? That it is rooted in the inherent, narcissistic contradictions of an arrested Oedipal complex? That it
is suffused with people bent on pursuing an impossible
resolution of what they necessarily feel to be a gender
deficiency? Not exactly. The most likely explanation for
certain kinds of sexual pathologies—particularly those
related to promiscuity, sexual objectification, and persis-
tent sexual dissatisfaction—is that male homosexual society is, well, male.

It is, indeed, almost alarming how much evolutionary
psychology can predict about gay and lesbian culture.
There is an old joke that Deborah Blum cites that brings
the point home. It goes: What does a lesbian bring on her
second date? A U-Haul. What does a gay man bring on his
second date? What second date? The reason, in other
words, that the reparative therapists are uninterested
in lesbianism is that the state of lesbian society would

undermine a critical element in their case for the inherent pathology of homosexuality. If anything, lesbian relationships sometimes suffer from a surfeit of intimacy and commitment, occasionally breaking down because the women involved overwhelm each other with mutual concern and enmeshment. If homosexual pathology is defined as an inability to bond in a stable relationship, then lesbianism, and not psychoanalysis, might seem to be the "cure."

Indeed, the nature of gay male society is far more persuasively explained—and understood—in terms of its gender than of its orientation. The landscape of gay life is, indeed, almost a painting in testosterone. There is much male posturing and competition; intense sexual rivalry, and the constant threat of infidelity. There is also an extraordinary devotion to male sexual display, from the carved gym physiques to the acute awareness of clothes. In a world where simple physical aggression does not easily work in the sexual game, where both the sexual prey and predator are males, competition can take many subtle forms and find itself expressed in the manipulation of money, power, fame, looks, or reputation. And it is a culture more instinctively sexualized than others, and more prey to disease. Men, after all, are both physically stronger and yet more vulnerable than women. They die younger; their sexual adventurism leads them into more risk; their competitiveness can engender dangerous behavior; and they are often more emotionally volatile, especially when young. All these things are true of heterosexual men. They are no truer of gay men, but, because their culture is often devoid of the presence of women, these characteristics are often exaggerated and intensified. Think of the competitive cult of sexual conquest of the 1970s—which ended in a viral catastrophe. Think also of the quest for the perfect body in the 1990s—which results in the steroidal grotesqueries of circuit culture. Sexual moderation does not come easily or spontaneously to men, whatever their orientation. How much less powerful an influence it is when women are hardly present at all.

And there is a twist to this as well. The greater levels of aggression and competitiveness among males also undoubtedly intensify the social pressures on the pre-homosexual boy far more than on a similarly aged pre-lesbian girl. If he markedly diverges in his behavior from many of his peers, their rejection is likely to be more severe and their aggression more intense. The evolutionary pressures that have led males to be more concerned with territory, physical aggression, and rivalry and status combine to impose often intolerable stress on a young, nonconforming boy.

Think of the way, for example, in which a soccer-playing girl is treated in our culture, as compared with, say, a ballet-dancing boy. In today's climate, she may even be celebrated as a sports star and supported with enthusiasm by both her parents. But the ballet-dancing boy will rarely enjoy comparable encouragement from either his family or his peers, especially the men and boys in his life. He will be cut off more severely, his identity framed and defined more inflexibly. So his conflicts may be deeper, and his later pathologies and dysfunctions therefore less malleable than a gender-nonconforming girl. It is no surprise, then, that pre-homosexual boys are more likely to commit suicide than pre-lesbian girls (and far more likely than pre-heterosexual boys); that adult gay men may exhibit greater rigidity in their sexual orientation than lesbian women; and that adult gay men may also suffer from more severe psychological problems. These facts, the evolutionary psychologists might suggest, are rooted in the more rigid, competitive and aggressive gender into which he is born.

But the corollary to this, of course, is lesbian culture, where dysfunction seems far less common, and social disapproval somewhat less intense. Legal sanctions against lesbianism have historically been less widespread than those against male homosexuality, and visceral loathing of lesbianism, especially among heterosexual men, is less open and common than hatred and fear of male homosexuals. There are more openly lesbian women in our society in positions of prominence than openly gay men; and although they endure a hefty amount of social disapproval and isolation, the boundaries between them and heterosexual women seem often far less rigid than those between gay and straight men.

In lesbian culture also, many of the alleged pathologies most closely associated with gay men seem to be absent. Personal competition sometimes cedes to an almost stifling emphasis on consensus and conformity; loving relationships are often the rule rather than the exception; sexual intrigue and the linkages between friends and lovers are complex and long-lasting. Here is a culture of extraordinary stability and variety, a monogamist's dream of political and social community which somehow has not found its champions among the family-mongering religious right.

It could be argued, of course, that this is precisely the reparative therapists' point: that both gay and lesbian cultures are dangerously unbalanced in different ways by their lack of gender integration. But it bears repeating that that is not the reparative therapists' point. Their point is that homosexual orientation—by the very nature of its psychological development—creates a pathology of sexual promiscuity and emotional dysfunction, and that such pathologies are inherent in the orientation, not contingent on the variable of gender. But if such pathologies exist (and, to a lesser extent, they do), they are far more plausibly explained by the social stigma attached from a very early age to the male homosexual and by the biological and cultural forces that, for good and ill, define his continued existence.

SO THE EMPIRICAL ANSWER to my adolescent question is, perhaps, clearer than the moral one. Homosexuality is not, in the usual sense of the word, normal. But nor is it, from a psychoanalytic context, necessarily abnormal. It is different. Because, in all likelihood, of a genetic predisposition and a unique set of early environmental influences, some boys and some girls grow up to become emotionally attracted to people of their own gender. It doesn't happen very often, and when it does, it is subject to a unique confluence of emotional, psychological circumstances that make every homosexual child as different from his peers as every heterosexual child. Although a war has been waged over this somewhat banal conclusion, it is difficult, it seems to me, to come to any other. We don't yet know the precise contours of this journey, but we know roughly where it goes.

And it is telling that this somewhat bathetic notion has proved, over time, to be so hard to absorb. The extreme defensiveness of homosexuals and their supporters, and the extreme hostility of the psychoanalytic experts, has conspired, over the years, to avoid it. And yet such an outcome hardly robs homosexuals of their integrity, or psychoanalysts of their usefulness. It is not, after all, necessary to be completely like everyone else to be accorded equal human dignity, and it is not necessary for people to be trapped in a vicious pathology to benefit from psychotherapy's insights.

So why the reluctance to embrace it? Perhaps because it threatens some of our most entrenched and entrenching patterns of thought. On the one hand, the resilience of homosexuality, despite social disapproval, despite religious hostility, despite massive social disincentives, and despite even a terrifying plague, mocks the aspirations of those who seek to impose order on a world where such order does not necessarily exist. On the other, the complexity of the roots of homosexuality, the fact that it may be a condition both imposed upon and created by homosexuals themselves, means that it cannot simply be debated like the color of a person's hair. Gay people would doubtless like the hair analogy to be accurate, because it would enable them to avoid the wrenching and often

painful self-analysis they would otherwise have to embark upon. But, alas, it isn't. And pain is, still, an ineluc-
table part of the examined homosexual life.

But the elusiveness of homosexuality is perhaps most
infuriating to those who would like to regulate, hide, or
eradicate it. The fact that it has often eluded the program-
matic attempts of so many people to impose a "natural"
order on society, and that it has slipped away from its
oppressors by force of irony, or humor, or bald courage, is a source of particular frustration. Even the most
partisan of the reparative therapists, for example, reluctantly acknowledge that their "treatment" is, more often
than not, unsuccessful. There is little reliable way independently to gauge their "conversion" success rate, but
even by their own reckoning, it is not so impressive. A
leading supporter of reparative therapy, Jeffrey Satinover,
reports that of those homosexuals most determined and
motivated to change their sexual orientation, embarking
on a rigorous program of psychoanalysis five times a
week, only a quarter make it into a marital relationship
with a member of the opposite sex. Socarides reports that
65 percent of his patients either discontinued treatment
or didn't finish it. Moreover, most of those who experience "successful" treatment do not eradicate homosexual
longing or desire; they merely seem able to supplement it
with heterosexual feelings, or at least do so enough to be
able to have relatively fulfilling relationships with members of the opposite sex.

A NARTH psychotherapist, Steven Richfield, has written that "even in the most ideal outcomes, it is my belief
that residual homosexual fantasies will emerge from time

to time throughout the lives of these men." In his view, "the most realistic goal of psychotherapy of ego-dystonic homosexuality [is] the growth of a strong masculine self-image that provides for a satisfying heterosexual adaptation which is not jeopardized by the periodic intrusion of homosexual fantasies." Richfield cites a quote from one such "success" case. His patient explains: "I've come to accept that there is a homosexual part inside of me that I may never be able to get rid of. But maybe I can learn to live with it. The other day I was at the swim club with my wife and sons. A man in a very tight bathing suit walked by and I caught myself staring and beginning to have fantasies. But just as quickly, I stopped myself, told myself it was not such a big deal, and dove in the water. And it didn't ruin my day."

It should be remembered that this kind of "success" is reported by those most interested in claiming the effectiveness of such therapy; that such therapy has been thoroughly repudiated by mainstream psychiatry and psychotherapy; that it occurs in those patients who are most conflicted about their sexual orientation and most motivated for therapeutic change; and that, even in the ideal scenario, it is obviously far from a cure. This suggests the extreme limits of this approach to the "problem" of homosexuality. If we generously accept the reparative therapists at their word that genuine therapeutic successes of this kind account for a quarter to a third of their cases, and also generously assume that their conflicted patients represent perhaps one in fifty homosexuals, then the best estimate of a "cure" rate for homosexuality as a whole, even under the most benign of circumstances, is less than 1 percent of the general homo-sexual population.

Perhaps in a totalitarian society where all known homosexuals were forced by law into reparative therapy, this number might be ratcheted up a little. But I doubt it would increase by much. And the most honest of the reparative therapists concede as much. They argue merely that their practice should be tolerated in a free society, and I see no reason why it shouldn't. No one should be stigmatized for making a genuine decision to try to alter his or her sexual orientation if it seems to be a source of immeasurable pain. And no therapist should be barred from giving such therapy. In a free society, such treatment would, I think, end up being, to coin a phrase, safe, legal, and rare. But it is surely no "solution," whatever such a word might mean in this context.

So when the opponents of reparative therapy describe its practitioners as purveyors of genocide, they are half right as well as half wrong. For such therapy is, in some ways, the ultimate incarnation of a way of thinking that sees the world as a set of problems to be solved. And with homosexuality, such therapy surely posits, if it doesn't achieve, a "final solution." It is both an attempt to define homosexuality in a definitive and expert fashion and an attempt to cure it at its source. But it has at first to nail the phenomenon down. And that, as Freud noticed, is remarkably difficult to do.

The most elegant metaphor for this elusive quality of homosexuality I know lies, fittingly enough, in a poem of W. H. Auden. Auden was trained as a geologist, and so it is appropriate that his analogy would be that of rock. In

"In Praise of Limestone," a poem pointed out to me by my friend Roy Tsao, Auden uses this particular rock as a metaphor for a resiliently subversive and elusive temperament. But it could also, I think, be seen as a metaphor for homosexuality itself. For Auden, homosexuality can be seen as having the quality of limestone, a porous rock that is malleable and unpredictable—and yet resistant:

> . . . Mark these rounded slopes
>   With their surface fragrance of thyme and, beneath,
> A secret system of caves and conduits; hear the springs
>   That spurt out everywhere with a chuckle,
> Each filling a private pool for its fish and carving
>   Its own little ravine . . .

This subversive, enchanting substance is not, Auden seems to say, easily admired by other soils. Granite wastes mock its impermanence and instability: "How evasive is your humor," they intone. "How accidental / Your kindest kiss, how permanent is death." An "oceanic whisper" insinuates to limestone that it cannot really know true emotional connection: "There is no love," it suggests. "There are only the various envies, all of them sad." And the clays and gravels impute to limestone a uselessness and impertinence which defies the work that needs always to be done:

> . . . "Come!" purred the clays and gravels,
> "On our plains there is room for armies to drill; rivers
> Wait to be tamed and slaves to construct you a tomb

In the grand manner: soft as the earth is mankind and both
Need to be altered."

What the existence of limestone suggests, of course, is that sometimes the world does not "need to be altered," sometimes its diversity and complexity and chaos are in fact not invitations to alteration but to acceptance. This rings so false to our rationalist world with its incessant "problems" and recurrent "solutions." But the endurance of homosexuality, the fact that it hovers precariously between nature and will, and that it posits a world where man's capacity to read order into nature may itself be untrue to nature, is a deep challenge to that rationalism. For it suggests that what might seem to be useless might actually have a use:

It has a worldly duty which in spite of itself
It does not neglect, but calls into question
All the Great Powers assume; it disturbs our rights.

This is not to endorse the idea that somehow homosexuality is defined by its otherness, by its intrinsic subversiveness, or by pathology. It is, rather, to resist the temptation to consign it either to otherness or to sameness, to normality or abnormality. It is neither a feature of utopia nor dystopia. Like all truly human phenomena, it belongs somewhere in between. For Auden, it partakes in normality and abnormality at one and the same time. Limestone, after all, while being radically different than other rocks, being even a rock that "dissolves in water," is still a rock. It is part of the landscape; it is nature of a different but wondrous kind, a kind that subverts even the notion of nature itself while giving brilliant and resilient homage to it.

Perhaps it is because this concept is so alien to our culture that homosexuals themselves have been so unable to embrace it. They have slipped into defining themselves either as completely interchangeable with heterosexuals or as utterly alien from them. And in the debate over the origins of homosexuality, they have found it very difficult to believe that they may indeed have become homosexual thanks, in part, to their early upbringing, to their mothers and fathers, and have found it even more difficult to own and accept that part of themselves without shame or defensiveness.

But why not? What ultimately could really be wrong with it? As long as homosexuality is intrinsically unrelated to pathologies that lead to unhappiness, why is such an emotional development so inferior to a heterosexual one? The only credible answer, I suppose, is because it might deny such people the same avenues of natural love that heterosexuals enjoy. But that is surely and patently untrue. For, in many ways, the resilience of homosexuality itself, its capacity to endure even against the most crippling discrimination, even against the most invasive psychotherapy, is ultimately not about the resilience of alienation, or subversion, or disease. It is about the resilience of love itself.

And it is one of the most telling features of reparative therapy that it so thoroughly denies the existence of anything that could be called homosexual love. It is indeed possible to read dozens of papers written by such thera-

pists (and "queer theorists" for that matter) without coming across the word at all. Again, Socarides is explicit:
"These homosexuals kid themselves and one another with
protestations of love and affection. Of course, they feel
something for their male lovers . . . [But] most, if not
all, homosexuals who say they are 'in love' are lying to
themselves." All their "love" amounts to, according to
Socarides, is a sublimated form of violence, selfishness,
and even incest.

It is, of course, vital for these architects of a cure to
deny the very existence of homosexual love. Because if it
did exist, they would have to confess that their project is,
in fact, what it is: an explicit attempt to destroy a deep,
human yearning for such love or to so direct it, through
extensive and invasive surgery, toward an object of which
they approve. They would have to confess that they are
surgeons of such love, exercising a power over the human
heart that only doctors hold over the human body.

But if anything, surely, should be safe from such surgery, it is love. Because love is intrinsically connected to
autonomy, because it is impossible to conceive of love
without also conceiving of choice, even foolish choice,
the attempt to eradicate or train or coerce it has long
been understood to be particularly corrosive of human
liberty. Which is why any society that seeks to stigmatize
or forbid love between two adult, unrelated beings is also
seeking to stigmatize and coerce a very basic form of
human liberty.

And it is not an argument against this to say that the liberty that love entails is always and everywhere a fickle liberty. It is precisely the fickle liberties that free societies

try most to protect. And love, indeed, has an infuriating tendency to pick an inappropriate object, to cut across barriers of class and race and gender, to threaten power with a more enduring and meaningful human relationship. It is no accident that societies have always attempted to coerce and channel and manipulate such an emotion and, indeed, to see it as the ultimate means to control human beings. And it is no accident that liberal societies have been the most adamant in protecting the instances of such love, in ensuring that its institutions (such as marriage) are available to all, and in worrying when government seeks to reorder or repress its manifestations. And insofar as homosexuality represents a peculiarly elusive instance of that love, its treatment is a critical indicator of the endurance of that liberty in a free society.

It is easy, indeed, to see why some people seek to deny that love's existence or to control its manifestation. For in controlling homosexuality, they control something far more common and far more threatening. Indeed, from being an undetectable, unmentionable love, homosexuality has slowly become a symbol of the subversive and transformative frontier of love as a whole, a sign not of dysfunction or disease but of liberty and self-knowledge. So it becomes more possible to understand what Auden really meant when he said that

> . . . when I try to imagine a faultless love
> Or the life to come, what I hear is the murmur
> Of underground streams, what I see is a limestone
> landscape.

3. IF LOVE WERE ALL

> And this is what we mean by friends: even when
> they are absent, they are with us; even when
> they lack some things, they have an abundance
> of others; even when they are weak, they are
> strong; and, harder still to say, even when they are
> dead, they are alive.
> —Cicero, *De Amicitia*

I DON'T THINK I'm alone in thinking that the deepest legacy of the plague years is friendship. The duties demanded in a plague, it turned out, were the duties of friends: the kindness of near strangers, the support that asks the quietest of acknowledgments, the fear that can only be shared with someone stronger than a lover. In this sense, gay men were perhaps oddly well prepared for the trauma, socially primed more than many others to face the communal demands of plague. Denied a recognized family, often estranged from their natural one, they had learned in the few decades of their free existence that friendship was the nourishment that would enable them to survive and flourish. And having practiced such a virtue in good times, they were as astonished as everyone else to see how well they could deploy it in bad.

It certainly came easily to me. For me, friendship has always been the most accessible of relationships—certainly far more so than romantic love. Friendship, I learned, provided a buffer in the interplay of emotions, a distance that made the risk of intimacy bearable, a space that allowed the other person to remain safely another person.

So, for most of my life, for a variety of reasons, I found it far simpler to make friends than to find lovers. No doubt, this had something to do with my homosexuality (since friendship is the only gay relationship that is socially acknowledged) and something to do with my haphazard romantic history (for want of a lover, a friend often filled the emotional spaces in my life). But friendship, although it may come more instinctively to some than to others, is not a relationship anyone has a special claim to. Gay men have sustained and nourished it in our culture only by default. And they are good at friendship not because they are homosexual, but because, in the face of a deep and silent isolation, they are human. Insofar as friendship was an incalculable strength of homosexuals during the calamity of AIDS, it merely showed, I think, how great a loss is our culture's general underestimation of this central human virtue.

For, of all our relationships, friendship is the most common and the most natural. In its universality, it even trumps family. Many of us fail to marry, and many more have no children; others never know their mother or father, and plenty have no siblings. But any human being who has ever lived for any time has had a friend. It is a relationship available to and availed by all of us. It is at once the most particular and the most universal relationship there is.

And yet we hardly talk about it. What we know most intimately in practice, we flee from in the abstract. The twentieth century has seen almost no theoretical exploration of friendship, no exposition of what it means, no defense of it, or even attack on it. Those modern writers who have ventured to deal with friendship have often done so in passing—a brief lecture by Kant, a diatribe by Kierkegaard, a sublime interlude by Oakeshott. The first and last serious treatment of the matter was Montaigne's, and even his landmark evocation, *"De l'Amitié,"* was a mere essay, and a tiny fraction of his total work. One has to journey far further back, to ancient and medieval times, to glimpse a world where this relationship was given its full due and seen as something worth examining in its own right—as a critical social institution, as an ennobling moral experience, as an immensely delicate but essential interplay of the virtues required to sustain a fully realized human being.

Of course, this modern silence may not be altogether a bad sign. There's something about friendship that lends itself to reticence. Lovers, after all, never stop telling each other about their love; they gabble endlessly about it, tell the world about it, emit excruciating poetry and a constant stream of art to reflect every small aspect of its power and beauty. But friends, more often than not, deflect attention from their friendship. They don't talk about it much. Sometimes, in fact, you can tell how strong the friendship is by the silence that envelops it. Lovers and spouses may talk frequently about their "relationship," but friends tend to let their regard for one another speak for itself or let others point it out.

And a part of this reticence is reflected in the moments when friendship is appreciated. If friendship rarely articulates itself when it is in full flood, it is often only given its due when it is over, especially if its end is sudden or caused by death. Suddenly, it seems, we have lost something so valuable and profound that we have to make up for our previous neglect and acknowledge it in ways that would have seemed inappropriate before. One of the greatest poetic expressions of friendship, perhaps, is Tennyson's "In Memoriam." The deepest essay, Montaigne's, was written about a friend who had been wrenched bitterly away from the author at an early age. Cicero's classic dialogue on the subject was written in honor of a dead friend; so was the most luminescent medieval work, Aelred of Rievaulx's *De Spirituali Amicitia.* Augustine's spasm of grief at the death of a friend is the first time he ever really expressed the friendship he once felt, rather than simply feeling it. And the emergence of friendship as a critical experience during the plague years merely confirms this pattern. It is as if death and friendship enjoy a particularly close relationship, as if it is only when pressed to the extremes of experience that this least extreme of relationships finds its voice, or when we are forced to consider what really matters, that we begin to consider what friendship is.

I FOUND MYSELF reading Augustine on a plane ride after Patrick's memorial service. There's something about the acute, accessible pain in Augustine's writing that has always made me feel less alone in moments of pain. And in the days after Pat's death, the grief had intensified. I had been eclipsed, it felt like, by a sudden sense of loss, a gloom made only more opaque by my confusion about what it actually was that I had lost. I felt as if I was in a dark room, kicking at a door that wasn't there. The dark-

ness went on immeasurably. It had no meaning that I
could decipher, and, although I had long anticipated it, it
still stung me. Augustine's account of his grief resonated
in a way nothing modern ever had. For this man, surely
one of the most remarkable men who has ever lived,
friendship was "sweet beyond all the sweetnesses of life
that I had experienced." Sweeter than love, than sex, than
physical pleasure, than all the sweetnesses of a carnal
world that he relished but was eventually, reluctantly,
to abandon. So when his friend died of a sudden illness,
his grief was of an intensity that today we reserve for our
family or spouses—not for those with whom we are
merely friends. This is how he put it:

> Grief darkened my heart. Everything on which I set
> my gaze was death. My home town became a torture
> to me; my father's house a strange world of unhappi-
> ness; all that I had shared with my friend was with-
> out him transformed into a cruel torment. My eyes
> looked for him everywhere, and he was not there. I
> hated everything because they did not have him, nor
> could they now tell me "look, he is on the way," as
> used to be the case when he was alive and absent
> from me . . . I found myself weighed down by a sense
> of being tired of living and scared of dying. I suppose
> the more I loved him, the more hatred and fear I felt
> for the death which had taken him from me, as if it
> were my most ferocious enemy. I thought that since
> death had consumed him, it was suddenly going to
> engulf all humanity.

It is only, perhaps, when you absorb the notion that someone is truly your equal, truly interchangeable with you, that the death of another makes mortality real. It is as if only in the death of a friend that a true reckoning with mortality is ever fully made, before it is too late, which is why so many theologians for so long saw friendship as an integral and vital part of a truly spiritual life. In that close encounter with the end of life, certain things become clearer before they become opaque again. And it is at these times that the feelings of grief may actually take the place of a friendship itself, providing a focus for attention, a physical and emotional catharsis that alone displaces the experience we recently had. Which is why we cling to it, like a narcotic, and are afraid of a normal future that will only remind us again of the loss that will never go away. With Patrick, death swept away the mystery of our friendship and exposed its raw existence. The friendship articulated itself at the moment that it ceased to exist.

We were as alike as we were unlike. Patrick was a big-boned, apple-cheeked, redheaded bruiser of a man, a Southerner with an immense capacity to charm and infuriate. My first sight of him (before I had ever met him) was watching him stride across Dupont Circle, shirtless, with a huge metal bicycle chain draped around his neck, like a python. I'd been told about him by a mutual friend, who'd known him since college and who thought we would get along. When I eventually got to know him, I began to see why. He had read everything, it seemed. All of Faulkner, twice over at least. Obscure works by Gide, and obscurer historical texts on the Civil War. He had taught himself to play the piano and relaxed listening to Marian McPartland and Arvo Pärt. Obsessed with food, he cooked vast, fatty, floury Southern meals, and knew Rilke in the original German. He laughed mischievously, made up stories, was prone to sudden violent outbursts of temper and hardly ever answered the phone. He was a deeply proud person, and fearless. A rebel who revered authority, a sexual adventurer who treasured love, a traditionalist who rarely gave up a chance to try something new, Patrick struck so many chords within me over the few years I knew him that it seemed truly as if the world were less lonely with him in it.

And to begin with, of course, I fell in love with him. Most of us did. He didn't allow many people into his intimate life, and the few of us who were privileged to be there were soon forced to tolerate some of the worst varieties of emotional manipulation, but we did so gladly. He drew us to him and kept us there, despite indignities, and rudenesses, and peremptory withdrawals. The charm was almost hypnotic, and there was a sweet serenity about it.

I met him in a bookstore, buying a dictionary. He had wandered over, mock sheepish, his shirt hanging out, his baggy khakis sliding down his rump. We struck up some inane conversation and exchanged phone numbers. Over the next few weeks, the courtship blossomed and collapsed. Our first date was an elaborate dinner, cooked in his apartment, accessible only by a fire escape which let into the kitchen itself. We got drunk and stuffed ourselves, and fooled clumsily around until it was time to go. I remember the large, old-fashioned candlewick bedspread he had, the kind my grandparents used to have, and the bric-a-brac he had collected from countless yard sales that was strewn around the place: plastic Madonnas, rural oil prints, a plaster sundial. And none of this was paraded as some sort of kitsch, an ironic statement of 1990s detachment. Everything Patrick collected he collected because it actually affected him, amused him, reflected some small part of a real and funny world he was glad to be a part of. The only thing Patrick was truly ironic about was irony. He would form his hands into the bunny ears of quotation marks and squawk his contempt.

Of course, he was already romantically involved (with more than one person, it turned out). And there came the inevitable moment when he had to tell me that our connection was about friendship not love, and that the kind of attachment I had begun to feel for him was something about which he could feel only ambivalence, not surety. He told me this on the street at night with tears in his eyes, his chubby face choking with sad transparency. In a world in which emotion is increasingly strained through the filter of self-mocking, Patrick never stinted in his feeling. It was direct and real and old. And his love was, at times, overpowering.

That love was no less love for being in the mode of friendship. We have come to dread that moment when a date or a lover turns to us and says, "Let's be friends," but this dread is too often a misplaced one. Patrick, in the first regard, taught me that. We would have been hopeless lovers: far too headstrong to tolerate each other's constant company, far too individual to have merged into one. But as friends, we had space to breathe, to be ourselves, and, by being ourselves in the company of each other, we helped each other ease more deeply into what we thought were our futures. We gave one other confidence, confidence to resist the categories into which society wanted to shoehorn us, confidence to risk too much in exploring our world, confidence to return to our somewhat estranged families and reconcile ourselves to their love.

The friendship had its ups and downs. One memorable explosion occurred when I blurted out the fact that Pat's ex-lover was now seeing someone else. Patrick fumed and then wrote the kind of letter that smokes in the mailbox. "Further, Andrew," his peroration climaxed, in a long and characteristically relentless screed, "your statement was accompanied by a gesture, a peculiarly self-satisfied, shit-eating smirk, clearly intended to vex, annoy, and upset." We didn't speak for a few weeks.

And the friendship had its unremarkable highs. There were many early evenings when, after a long and bruising day at work, I would simply arrive at Pat's, let myself in, lie down on his couch, and listen to a constant rush of increasingly far-fetched stories, about his life, his hometown, or the characters he had come across in his recent travels. These moments of calm, of unspoken informality, of unarticulated ease in each other's worlds, were, I think, characteristic of friendship, at least in its less developed form.

For months and then years, this friendship continued, occasionally fading and sometimes unexpectedly crackling. But then it changed, or slipped into another dimension, or intensified so dramatically that it seemed to take on a qualitatively different form. And it was almost as if we felt it coming. In the summer that I had been diagnosed with HIV, Patrick had momentarily disappeared. This wasn't particularly strange. For days and sometimes weeks at a time, Pat would simply drop out of sight, fail to return calls, or just absent himself from social duties. But this absence had come after a particularly difficult conversation we had just had. We had sat on the floor in my apartment and talked about the disease that stalked both of us. Pat rarely talked about it, and had never gotten tested. I had just gotten my results, and was still in shock. Fearful of telling anyone, I had even kept the news from Patrick. But I needed to be near him and to talk, even in code, about the fear that was consuming me.

I remember how hard it was to lie to him or not to tell him everything. For the first time in our friendship, I kept something back, pinioned by the disease, and the shame, and the terror of exposure, into compromising our mutual honesty, in protecting myself from my friend's protection. But he seemed intuitively to understand and, oddly enough, to talk about his own fears. "Sometimes," he said, "it feels like some bogeyman in the forest, waiting to pounce on my back, and sometimes I wish it would, just because then I'd know where it was. And I'd know how to fight it. It would be in front of me, and I'd know what to do. I really wish I had it, somehow. It would be less frightening than not knowing."

Within a few weeks of that conversation, Pat was hospitalized with AIDS-related pneumonia. I didn't know about his illness at first, because, like me, he decided to keep it to himself. In this, we both participated in one of the unsung rites of AIDS. Not so much the fear, or the shame, but the fusion of the two, the uniquely isolating and self-punishing crucible in which the disease often announces itself. But after a month or so of not seeing him, or getting my many calls returned, I spotted him in his usual place at Mass and noticed he looked remarkably thinner. When I tried to catch his eye, he bent down in prayer. And after Communion, after my own prayers, when I looked up to go to that part of the church to talk to him, he had suddenly disappeared. He was avoiding me.

Then, a few days later, he called me at my office and said he wanted to talk to me about something. It was serious, he said. I told him I wanted to talk to him too. I too had something difficult to tell him. There had been, for both of us, a slow erosion in the wall of discretion we had constructed between us. We met a few blocks away, at a fountain in a park, and told each other, with mounting disbelief, the same piece of news. And in the muggy haze of a Washington summer afternoon, the friendship began again. Whatever barriers and boundaries there had been between us until that moment suddenly dissolved into something much more like union, solidarity, relief. So much relief. We were at that moment each other's only HIV-positive friend, each other's only confidant in the same tribulation. And what we had previously had in common swiftly seemed trivial in comparison.

Pat wrote me later that summer about how he felt:

> With all that's happened to us—together and apart
> —I'm inclined to think that somehow we were
> chosen to know each other, to help sustain each
> other, and to teach each other about the mysteries

of loving, living, dying. After the initial crush of your news, when I had been prepared not to receive but to give a report on my HIV status to you, I found myself strangely grown more attached and connected to you, even protective of you, and I felt an effusion of love and tenderness that, for the first time since I met you, was not constrained by considerations of others, of anything or anyone other than you, and me, and our feelings for one another. Somehow I was able to love you wholly, and this gave me great strength to face the greatest fears I have known. How is it that such news can clear an immediate path between us, sweep away the debris and the impediments . . . ?

I don't know how the letter continued, because he never sent it to me, and that is the only page I have. It was found in his possessions a year or so after his death. Perhaps he felt it unnecessary in the end to say it to me and merely needed to prove it to himself. The reticence of friendship, again. Or perhaps the feeling was powerful and true only for that moment, and seemed excessive in retrospect. But it was, I think, nevertheless real, at least for a moment. And I felt it too.

THE ANCIENT GREEK word for friendship was a somewhat promiscuous thing. The Greeks called it *philia,* and it referred to a variety of relationships, small and large, virtuous and shallow. In the single greatest examination of friendship ever written, Aristotle's Books Eight and

Nine of the *Nicomachean Ethics,* the word covers a multitude of connections. In Aristotle's hermetically sane universe, the instinct for human connection is so common and so self-evidently good that there is little compunction to rule certain relationships out of the arc of human friendliness. There is merely an attempt to understand and categorize each instance of *philia* and to place each instance of the instinct in its natural and ennobling place. Everything is true, Aristotle seems to say, so long as it is never taken for anything more than it is. And so friendship belongs to the nod of daily passengers on a commuter train, to the regular business client, and to the ornery neighbor. It encompasses the social climber and the social butterfly, the childhood crush and the lifelong soulmate. It comprises the relationship between a boss and his employees, a husband and a wife, a one-night stand and a longtime philanderer, a public official and his dubious contributor.

And it is, for Aristotle, a shockingly important phenomenon. The nature of friendship takes up a full fifth of his entire account of human ethical conduct. Romantic love—an experience which we moderns have elevated to the height of our aspirations and concerns—is subsumed as almost a footnote. Family relationships are also folded into a subcategory of *philia,* and not a particularly significant one. Friendship, in contrast, is the pre-eminent human experience. It is more important than wealth, than honor, even more primary than justice:

> For friendship is some sort of excellence or virtue, or involves virtue, and it is, moreover, indispensable for life. No one would choose to live without friends,

even if he had all other goods. Rich men and those who hold office and power are, above all others, regarded as requiring friends. For what good would their prosperity do them if it did not provide them with the opportunity for good works? And the best works done and those which deserve the highest praise are those that are done to one's friends . . . When people are friends, they have no need of justice, but when they are just, they need friendship in addition. In fact, the just in the fullest sense is regarded as constituting an element of friendship . . .

Friendship, for Aristotle, seems to be the cornerstone of human society and flourishing, an integral part of happiness, and bound up inextricably with the notion of virtue. It is almost, it seems, prior to the notion of the individual himself. Just as, for Aristotle, human beings are somehow not human beings unless they are part of a social network, so human beings cannot be fully themselves without the opportunity to befriend and to enjoy the activity of being with friends. It is as fundamental to his understanding of what it is to be human as eating and drinking and breathing.

So the modern conflict between the self and others, the struggle with intimacy and interaction, the necessity for privacy and boundaries, doesn't really emerge in Aristotle's world. What we have, instead, is an ease with human relationships, and an attempt merely to articulate their proper ordering. For if Aristotle is promiscuous in his use of the term *philia*, he is hardly undiscriminating in its various expressions. Some forms of friendship are clearly

preferable to others. So Aristotle famously divides friendship into three categories: friendship based on what is
pleasant, friendship based on what is useful, and friendship based on what is good. And there is little doubt
which is the pre-eminent one.

We have all experienced friendships of pleasantness,
although we may not be particularly proud of them. I
realized one day that many of my friends were actually
good-looking, and that, although many of them had other
attractive characteristics, I was not exactly indifferent
to their physical appearance. There are, alternatively,
people who are merely witty, or funny, or have a quality
about them that somehow amuses you. Hanging out with
such people is an inherently pleasurable experience; it
may make you feel better about yourself, or it may
merely abate the encroaching boredom of things. But it
is based upon something that is essentially superficial,
if real. Aristotle points out how common this kind of
friendship is among the young. And how it also lies
behind the experience—more common among the young
than among the old—of "falling in love":

> Friendships of young people seem to be based on
> pleasure. For their lives are guided by emotion,
> and they pursue most intensely what they find
> pleasant and what the moment brings . . . Hence
> they become friends quickly and just as quickly
> cease to be friends. For as another thing becomes
> pleasant, the friendship, too, changes, and the plea-
> sure of a young man changes quickly. Also, young
> people are prone to fall in love, since the greater

part of falling in love is a matter of emotion and based on pleasure. That is why they form a friendship and give it up again so quickly that the change often takes place within the same day . . .

Notice how Aristotle condescends to these kinds of friendships but how he also gives them their due. They are real connections, and human beings are attracted to the pleasant and the beautiful. They are also attracted to the useful. These "useful" relationships are built upon the notion that one of the parties brings one thing to the contract, and the other party brings another. So a wealthy older man snags a younger trophy wife: the *philia* there is built on a trade of money for beauty. The wife gets money; the husband gets a livelier sex life and bragging rights. Or a smart but nerdy student is befriended by the college football star. One gets his papers written for him; the other gets to accompany the social star to an occasional frat party. Or a dumb but presentable politician hires an obscure but brainy academic. One gets a patina of seriousness; the other gets a buzz from power. It's a trade. For Aristotle, these friendships are real, and they deserve the name of friendship, but they are fundamentally dependent on the stability of the goods each party brings to the relationship, and so can disappear as quickly as they arise. If the trophy wife ages and her beauty fades, then she is liable to be dumped for the next package of glamour; and if her husband loses his money in a stock slump, then she may be tempted to shop elsewhere for her financial security.

And there is an element of this in much subtler relationships, friendships that are, on the surface, genuine but conceal beneath a welter of competing interests and advantages. How many of us, for example, are more diligent about those friendships that give us cachet, or access, or security, or a reflected sense of self-worth, than those (if they exist) that give us none of these things? Aristotle sees these mixed motives but understands them as simply part of human life. Pure connections are very rare, he seems to imply. For most of us, friendship is an alloyed experience, muddied with pleasure and need and mere amusement. In the *Rhetoric*, Aristotle lists some qualities which are worth having in friends. They do not make for a very enlightening set of characteristics, but they are highly recognizable. We are friends, he says, with

> those who are pleasant to pass the time with and spend our days with. These are good-tempered types, not eager to expose our mistakes, not competitive, and not quarrelsome . . . They are dexterous in making jokes and taking them . . . We are also friendly to people who praise the good points we have, especially those who praise the ones we think we lack . . . Also to those who do not make us feel ashamed of doing something unconventional—provided that this is not because we do not look down on them— and to those who make us feel ashamed of doing what is really wrong.

With that final, surprising twist, we arrive at what Aristotle defines as true friendship. Suddenly, it seems, we do not merely have the capacity to be friends with beauties and rationalizers, jokers and daredevils, but also with someone who is concerned with what is good and what is true. And this, for Aristotle, constitutes the third and critical type of friendship, the only friendship that lasts and the friendship that is the essential complement to the person of virtue and wisdom. But it isn't the only type of friendship, as we've seen. It is different from the friendships of taste and usefulness only in degree, and not, it seems, in kind.

To become a friend with someone who is truly virtuous takes time, because it takes time to figure out exactly how virtuous he is. "The wish to be friends can come quickly," as Aristotle nicely puts it, "but friendship cannot." In this pure form of friendship, pleasantness is present but incidental; it flows from the virtue of the relationship and is not the reason for the relationship in the first place. And usefulness as a motive and as a basis for connection is abandoned. Someone is not a true friend because it is useful for him; he is a friend in order that he might be useful for someone else.

But friendship is not a selfless act. For Aristotle, friendship is a natural emanation of self-love. In fact, it is impossible without self-love. If a man cannot love himself, if his mind and spirit are not in equilibrium, if his desires are not moderated by prudence and his passions not filtered by his rationality, then he is essentially incapable of the truest form of friendship. Before modern psychologists developed the concept of "co-dependency," Aristotle was alert to its dangers. For "a man is his own best friend," and everything a virtuous man does is ultimately for his own sake. He is not reaching out of himself to another person; he is not trying to compensate for his own sense of inadequacy by attracting others, or idolizing them, or throwing himself into their lives. He gives of himself freely, and in the ultimate form of friendship, he only befriends someone who is equally free in his capacity for friendship, and equally in love with himself.

This is not the same as manic egoism, narcissism, or selfishness, although it's hard not to sense a certain smugness in Aristotle's ideal human. A man in control of himself will often do extraordinarily generous things for his friends—"he will freely give his money, honors, and, in short, all good things that men compete for, while he gains nobility for himself"—but this is all a mere reflection of his own virtue which is, in the ultimate analysis, good for him. In Aristotle, there is no modern, irreconcilable conflict between what is virtuous and what is pleasant, between what is good for a person and what is moral, or between what a man wants to do and what will make him happy. A virtuous man is a man who is in balance, and he is happy, and his life is pleasant, and his capacity for friendship with others is a simple and elegant extension of his own easy self-regard.

If these are the types of friendship available to us, Aristotle has yet to say what it is that they all have in common, what is, in some sense, definitive of friendship itself. And the closest Aristotle comes to pinning down that elusive quality is a list of conditions. A friendship, to be a friendship, he argues, has to be a reciprocal relationship, it has to be between equals, and it has to be between people who physically share each other's lives.

At first blush, like many arguments in Aristotle, these

conditions might seem obvious, even banal. But on closer inspection, they prove more nettlesome. Why, for instance, to take the last condition, should two friends have to spend their lives together? Perhaps the central quality of some of my oldest friendships is that they have endured long periods of being apart. A really good friend, indeed, might be defined as someone whom you need not see for a year or so, or even longer, and yet, when you next get together, it is as if nothing has happened. The relationship snaps instantly back into place, as if the year were a matter of hours. The mutual understanding and trust are such that they don't require constant tending or proximity. But we may, of course, be deluding ourselves, Aristotle seems to imply. Perhaps the friendship we think we still have is actually a friendship that once existed and is now a delusion, viable for a few hours of conversation but, if tested, very fragile and easily broken if subjected to a new period of intense cohabitation. Sometimes, these friendships are not truly friendships; they are memories of friendships, carefully draped around our shoulders like old college scarves that have only a nostalgic meaning in our adult lives. The trust may indeed be the same; even the rapport. But friendship, Aristotle seems to say, is premised on an activity. It has to be practiced to truly exist. It is not merely a feeling. It is a behavior. It is bound up with the desire of two people to be together in some sort of common activity or to share life. How can it really have meaning if those people do not have some physical or verbal contact on a regular basis? It has been said that a person's religion is best defined not by what he says he believes but simply by what he actually does. Equally, it could be said that one's friends are simply those people with whom one spends one's life. Period. Anything else is a form of rationalization.

Reciprocity, perhaps, is an easier concept to swallow. Unlike a variety of other relationships, friendship requires an acknowledgment by both parties that they are involved or it fails to exist. One can admire someone who is completely unaware of our admiration, and the integrity of that admiration is not lost; one may even employ someone without knowing who it is specifically one employs; one may be related to a great-aunt whom one has never met (and may fail ever to meet). And one may, of course, fall in love with someone without the beloved being aware of it or reciprocating the love at all. And in all these cases, the relationships are still what they are, whatever the attitude of the other person in them: they are relationships of admiration, business, family, or love.

But friendship is different. Friendship uniquely requires mutual self-knowledge and will. It takes two competent, willing people to be friends. You cannot impose a friendship on someone, although you can impose a crush, a lawsuit, or an obsession. If friendship is not reciprocated, it simply ceases to exist or, rather, it never existed in the first place. This is one of the aspects that distinguishes it from, say, affection. One may feel affection for an inanimate object, or a distant acquaintance, or a character in a soap opera. And it is not necessary for them to feel any affection back for the emotion to be true and genuine. But friendship is defined by the reciprocation of such an emotion, not the emotion itself. And there may be times when the emotions which constitute the activity of friendship change dramatically—from warmth to frustration, from passion to anger, from coldness to irritation. But what defines the friendship is not any of these emotions but the primary, and always reciprocated, commitment to the other person. So, as Aristotle acutely observes, friendship is not an emotion but a "characteristic or lasting attitude." And it has to be mutual—even in its most mundane form. If the old lady on the bus fails to return your morning nod, then she is either losing her eyesight or you are, unfortunately, no longer friends.

But the central condition of friendship—and it is a condition echoed throughout the centuries of argument about the phenomenon—is equality between the parties. Again, this may seem a banal point on the surface, but the more you think about it, the more significant it seems. It is linked to reciprocity. Because each human being is equal in his capacity to assent or not to assent to a relationship, each is, in some sense, radically equal in the capacity for friendship. Even in relationships in which one person vastly outweighs the other in money, or wit, or good looks, or social power, the inferior party can quit the friendship of his own accord and reduce it to its essential elements. A friendship is thus ultimately defined by the desire of each person to be in it. And it is successful insofar as that desire is equal between the two parties.

But does it cease to exist when those desires are unbalanced? Aristotle, in his expansiveness, suggests not. He is, as we've seen, extremely generous in his definitions of what may be a friendship. So in friendships where one partner is far more admirable than the other, Aristotle merely urges that the relationship proportionally reflect the imbalance, thus somehow equalizing it. So if a very virtuous man befriends a less virtuous man, the friendship will work out as long as the less enlightened character doles out more admiration than his superior. Here, it seems, equal respect would actually unbalance the relationship. And in the last resort, Aristotle seems to say, you do what you can: "Friendship demands the possible; it does not demand what the giver deserves."

But, however imperfect the practice, what is clear is that the central principle of friendship is a form of equality. Unlike many relationships which are essentially unequal—master-slave, father-son, and (for Aristotle) husband-wife—friendship is essentially equal. If it fails to achieve that equality easily, it might endure after a fashion, but accommodations must nevertheless be made in accordance with the principle of equality, which gives it meaning. And it reaches its apogee when two equals come together, especially two virtuous equals. Then and only then do we see the perfect form of friendship flourish and take hold. It is the ideal toward which all the other human messes gravitate.

This, of course, is a highly subversive notion and not, on reflection, self-evident. Why, after all, should equality be the goal of the supreme human connection? Why would we not be more satisfied in a relationship of domination, or of cruelty, or of power? It's especially striking in Aristotle, who can hardly be seen as an apostle of radical equality. And yet Aristotle sees friendship as a remarkable solvent in human affairs, able to transcend a variety of social structures and resistant even to the most constrictive of natural limitations. Friendship, it seems, is almost a central symbol of human autonomy, and the most accessible example of that autonomy in practice.

For Aristotle, after all, friendship, although it is at its most sublime among virtuous and educated gentlemen, is still possible throughout a society, between men and women, between adults and children, even between free men and slaves. Friendship between a citizen and a slave might be thought of at first blush as impossible, but this is only partly true: "Inasmuch as a slave is a slave, there can be no friendship with him, but there can be friendship with him as a man. For there seems to be some element of justice in any human being's relationship to a man capable of sharing in law and contract. Therefore, friendship, too, is possible with him inasmuch as he is a human being." *Inasmuch as he is a human being.* In those words, we see a principle, even in the undemocratic political thought of Aristotle, of the essential equality of all people; and it is friendship, and the capacity for friendship, that paves the way.

THE GREAT MODERN ENEMY of friendship has turned out to be love. By love, I don't mean the principle of giving and mutual regard that lies at the heart of friendship. And I don't mean what Saint Paul meant by love, the Christian notion of indiscriminate and universal *agape* or *caritas,* which is based on the universal love of the Christian God. I mean love in the banal, ubiquitous, compelling, and resilient modern meaning of love: the romantic love that obliterates all other goods, the love to which every life must apparently lead, the love that is consummated in sex and celebrated in every particle of our popular culture, the love that is institutionalized in marriage and instilled as a primary and ultimate good in every Western child. I mean *eros*, which is more than sex but is bound up with sex. I mean the longing for union with another being, the sense that such a union resolves the essential quandary of human existence, the belief that only such a union can abate the loneliness that seems to come with being human, and deter the march of time that threatens to trivialize our very existence.

The centrality of this love in our culture is so ingrained that it is almost impossible to conceive of a world in which it might not be so. And this is strange in a society in which the delusions and dangers of such love are all around us: the wreckage of many modern marriages, the mass of unwanted pregnancies, the devastation of AIDS, the social ostracism of the single and the old. Even those sources of authority that might once have operated as a check on this extraordinary cultural pre-eminence have caved in to the propaganda of *eros*. The Christian churches, which once wisely taught the primacy of *caritas* to *eros*, and held out the virtue of friendship as equal to the benefits of conjugal love, are now our culture's primary and obsessive propagandists for the marital unit and its capacity to resolve all human ills and satisfy all human needs. Far from seeing divorce and abortion and sexual disease as reasons to question our society's apotheosis of *eros*, these churches see them merely as opportunities to intensify the idolatry of *eros* properly conducted and achieved. We live in a world, in fact, in which respect and support for *eros* has acquired all the hallmarks of a cult. It has become our civil religion.

And, of course, the attraction of romantic love is not hard to understand. While it lasts, which generally isn't for long, it can eclipse every other emotion and transport us to levels of bliss and communion we have never felt before. It is intoxicating, but, unlike most other forms of intoxication, it appears to have meaning and depth. We believe, for a moment, that we have found our lost soulmate, that we are reunited with another half of ourselves that finally gives meaning to everything in our lives. And because we are with that person, more often than not gazing into his or her eyes, it is easy and indeed necessary to abandon perspective. In fact, it almost seems a crime against love to retain any sort of perspective. Uniquely among human experiences, *eros* gives us the courage to say that such normal or habitual concerns are ultimately irrelevant; indeed almost anything is irrelevant—even time, even death—in the face of love's demands. This is why lovers will pretend that their love is eternal, and indeed insist upon it, because to trap it in time would be to impair the inherently unbounded nature of the experience. And it is why they say they are prepared to die for one another, or that they cannot live without one another, because anything else implies that love is just one competing good among others. But love is a supremely jealous thing. It brooks no rival and obliterates every distraction. It seems to transport the human being—who is almost defined by time and mortality—beyond the realm of both age and death. Which is why it is both so irresistible and so delusory.

Almost every serious thinker before Rousseau took these commonplace observations for granted. Love, it was understood, was based first and foremost on the beautiful, rather than the good. It captivated the eyes before it captured the soul. And as such, it was particularly superficial and fleeting and fragile. Beauty declines; youth corrupts. It is one thing to try to capture and enjoy such beguiling goods; it is another to pretend that they are somehow eternal. But everything about love is suffused with this kind of paradox. Even the promise of bodily and spiritual union in *eros* is self-delusory. For bodies cannot, strictly speaking, unite. They can merely entwine, or interpenetrate, or embrace. Although lovers will often say they want to devour each other, to absorb each other, to feel their bodies in and under each other's skin, to become each other, they cannot obviously achieve any of this, except superficially and for a few nanoseconds. But they embark on the impossible and pretend it is everything their lives have been leading to, and they throw themselves into the temporary while claiming it is forever. Is it any wonder, then, that the inevitable arrival of love's dissolution is as ritualized in our culture as the ecstatic moments of its awakening?

Of course, the impossibility of love is partly its attraction. It is an irrational act, a concession to the passions, a willing renunciation of reason and moderation—and that's why we believe in it. It is also why, in part, the sober writers and thinkers of the ancient and medieval worlds found it a self-evidently inferior, if bewitching, experience. But their confidence in this regard was based not simply on a shrewd analysis of love but on a deeper appreciation of friendship. Without the possibility of friendship, after all, love might seem worth the price. If the promise of union, of an abatement to loneliness, of finding a soulmate, was only available through the vagaries of *eros,* then it might be worth all the heartbreak and insanity for a glimpse, however brief, of what makes life worth living. But if all of these things were available in a human relationship that is not inherently self-destructive, then why, after all, should one choose the riskier and weaker option?

And in almost every regard, friendship delivers what love promises but fails to provide. The contrasts between the two are, in fact, many, and largely damning to love's reputation. Where love is swift, for example, friendship is slow. Love comes quickly, as the song has it, but friendship ripens with time. If love is at its most perfect in its infancy, friendship is most treasured as the years go by. Allan Bloom has pointed out the joke at the heart of arguably the greatest depiction of romantic love in our literature, *Romeo and Juliet.* At the very beginning of the play, Romeo is obsessed with a beautiful girl, and cannot get her out of his head. His friends make fun of his insistence on capturing her, and his inability to think of anyone else. The name of the girl? Rosaline. The greatest romantic hero of all time, the man whom one associates always with eternal love, was, in fact, obsessed with another woman just minutes before his first meeting with Juliet. This, Shakespeare seems to tell us, is the very nature of love. It is, at its root, meaningless and random. It can switch its object at the drop of a hat. And it can be fastened onto someone we cannot know and hardly understand. But Romeo, in his way, understands it:

> *Love is a smoke rais'd with the fume of sighs;*
> *Being purg'd, a fire sparkling in lovers' eyes;*
> *Being vex'd, a sea nourish'd with lovers' tears:*
> *What is it else? a madness most discreet,*
> *A choking gall, and a preserving sweet.*

And this discreet madness is at first evoked by Rosaline, before, within a matter of days, it is bestowed on Juliet, and with a surety that will lead both of the young lovers to their early and tragic deaths. Shakespeare's brilliance is to make us see the madness of their passion—and its superficiality—while also showing us its beauty and power. It is no accident, I think, that Romeo's greatest friend, Mercutio, is killed before the love affair can truly take off. It is love, Shakespeare teaches us, that supplants friendship, but friendship that is based on what is truer. Shakespeare lived in a world which had not yet raised *eros* to a supreme principle, and so he could retain a modicum of condescension to it, as well as awe.

If love is sudden, friendship is steady. At the moment of meeting a friend for the first time, we might be aware of an immediate "click" or a sudden mutual interest. But we don't "fall in friendship." And where love is often at its most intense in the period before the lover is possessed, in the exquisite suspense of the chase, and the stomach-fluttering nervousness of the capture, friendship can only really be experienced when both friends are fully used to each other. For friendship is based on knowledge, and love can be based on mere hope. Love, as Aquinas noticed, is part of the appetitive instinct; friendship is part of the contemplative. You can love someone more than you know him, and he can be perfectly loved without being perfectly known. But the more you know a friend, the more a friend he is.

Whereas love lives often in the future, a future of breathless possibilities masked in a stunning, rapturous present, friendship draws strength from the past, from myriad shared jokes and understandings, from the remembrance of moments endured or celebrated together, especially the small ones. Friends, as the poet J. D. McClatchy put it,

> are fables of our loneliness.
> If love would live for hope, friendship thrives
> On memory, the friends we "make" made up
> Of old desires for surprise without danger,
> For support without a parent's smarting ruler,
> For a brother's sweaty hand and a trail of crumbs.

When a friend is apart from a friend, she doesn't desperately need her, feel abandoned without her, unable to conceive of a future without her presence. She merely misses her, misses what her presence does for her, misses the familiarity that builds friendship, like a predictable tide builds dunes. Love affairs need immense energy, they demand a total commitment and a capacity for pain. Friendship, in contrast, merely needs tending. Although it is alive, a living, breathing thing, and can suffer from neglect, friendship can be left for a while without terrible consequences. Because it is built on the accumulation of past experiences, and not the fickle and vulnerable promise of future ones, it has a sturdiness that love may often lack, and an undemonstrative beauty that love would walk heedlessly past.

And part of this sturdiness comes from a similarity between friends. Friends, of course, can be very different from one another—in temperament and interests, character and virtue. But all their differences merely provide a context for their sameness. However different they are, when they interact as friends, they do so from a position of being alike. If they did not have this similarity, the friendship could not exist. I think this is what Aristotle was getting at with his insistence on equality, even amid inequality. However different the two friends, something similar must unite them, and the core of their friendship rests in that similarity. In the least profound friendships, this may merely be a similar interest—skiing or history, country houses or shopping. But in the deepest friendships, what is shared is something more profound. Two people share the same principles, or search for the same truth, or engage life with the same seriousness. And they are friends, even though they may lead dramatically different lives, to the extent that they are on the same path with the same intent.

Love, in contrast, is all about difference. Evolutionary psychologists tell us we are driven by a need to find a mate of as strikingly a different genetic makeup as possible. Sex, we are informed, is about the unification of difference, for the betterment of the species. But even without science, we know this to be true. When Shakespeare brought a

Montague and a Capulet together in the story of *Romeo and Juliet,* he was not merely constructing a plot device. Opposites, as we know, attract. When the purest love must be evoked, artists portray it between two poles of otherness, of class or race, background or religion, character or type. This difference is somehow intrinsic to the experience. The vast majority of lovers, after all, are of different genders, and even homosexual lovers seek to encounter a human other, to discover a difference and explore it. The exotic is often erotic, and the incongruity of two lovers is often proof to them of their destiny.

Yes, many marital partners come from the same class and background. But, then, many marriages (at least the ones that last) are not based on *eros.* Most love affairs, by definition, are. And they thrive upon conflict and misunderstanding and otherness. Indeed, part of the attraction of true love is that it can overcome radical difference and make it irrelevant. "It makes no sense," we say in love. "And that's why I trust it." In fact, the prototypical act of a truly erotic relationship is the frenzy of lovemaking that follows a brutal fight: it is a symbol of difference, overcome and intensified by longing. To be sure, most relationships are not entirely like this; they contain elements of friendship as much as love. But insofar as they reflect the essence of *eros,* they are filled with polarity. And just as friends can be very different people but, in their friendship, alike, so lovers can be very similar people but, in their love, different. That, after all, is partly what turns us on.

Maybe this helps explain why friendships seem more common and more natural between members of the same gender. A different gender inevitably separates people, which is why it hinders friendship among men and women and encourages love to breach the gap. Similarly, a shared experience of maleness or femaleness gives friends of the same gender an automatic beginning, a biological and cultural likeness that is peculiarly fertile territory for friendship to flourish. I don't mean to imply that the pressure of gender makes male-female friendships impossible, merely that it makes them rarer, and always susceptible to the destabilizing force of love. A man and a woman may come together as friends in a shared enterprise or passion; they may strive for the same goals or merely delight in each other's company or intelligence. But if this is to work, they have to put the temptation of *eros* behind them, by satiating it or renouncing it or by turning sex into an expression of friendship, rather than love. This describes, in many respects, the most successful marriages, where the original spark of *eros* has slowly lit a flame of *philia* that sustains the union when other more compelling passions have long since died away. Indeed, one of the least celebrated but most important achievements of the increasingly successful battle for women's equality is that it has properly expanded the universe of friendship for both men and women and made marriage more of a setting for friendship than for love. This is no mean accomplishment.

And this is also why sex between friends is something to be avoided at all costs: for sex, in its full penetrative sense, is a physical enactment of an emotional decision; it signals the congress of two different beings, a resolution of the distinctness on which friendship relies. C. S. Lewis wrote that the prototypical stance of two lovers is facing one another, their eyes gazing at each other, enraptured in each other's selves. But the classic stance of two friends is side by side, looking ahead in the same direction. The two stances are not complementary; they are opposed. And although it is conceivable to unite them, it is quite a hazardous enterprise. When a friendship becomes a love, of course, the moment may be particularly liberating. But it is liberating precisely because one is leaving the distance and discipline that friendship demands for the union and abandon that love promises.

For love is about control and loss of control. In love, we give ourselves up to each other. We lose control or, rather, we cede control to another, trusting in a way we would never otherwise trust, letting the other person hold the deepest part of our being in their hands, with the capacity to hurt it mortally. This cession of control is a deeply terrifying thing, which is why we crave it and are drawn to it like moths to the flame, and why we have to trust it unconditionally. In love, so many hazardous uncertainties in life are resolved: the constant negotiation with other souls, the fear and distrust that lie behind almost every interaction, the petty loneliness that we learned to live with as soon as we grew apart from our mother's breast. We lose all this in the arms of another. We come home at last to a primal security, made manifest by each other's nakedness.

I'm not saying that all love is like this or that every affair is defined by this kind of mutual surrender. But I am saying that this is the principle to which all love finally pays homage, the criterion by which such relationships are ultimately to be judged. It is, of course, a sublime experience, almost inhuman, because it is about the loss of the self-control which ultimately makes us who we are. And with that loss of control comes mutual power, the power to calm, the power to redeem, and the power to hurt. In some relationships, one partner holds that ultimate power, and the love is unequal. But in those relationships, the other partner must want to be powerless, yearn to be controlled or held, if the underlying principle of love is not to be undermined. And in other relationships, the power is distributed and redistributed from day to day and hour to hour and, sometimes, minute to minute. It will always differ, of course, in how it is given expression. But the principle is the same: it is a principle of control, of giving and retaining it, of wielding and begging for it. It is a strange mix of choice and unchoice, of the ultimate control and ultimate loss of control.

Perhaps Freud understood the depth and power of this impulse better than anyone. He saw it as related to that primal need, of a child for its parents, and to the delirious security of a parent's total control, mitigated only by a parent's total love. But, of course, no lover loves as a mother loves her child; it is always a simulacrum of that primal care, a delusory re-enactment that is as doomed as it is irresistible. Still, is it any mystery why we are compelled toward it, sensing in it a fulfillment lost even to our own memory but promising a final resolution to our crippling human need?

Nothing could be more unlike friendship. A condition of friendship is the abdication of power over another, indeed the abdication even of the wish for power over one another.

And one is drawn to it not by need but by choice. If love is about the bliss of primal unfreedom, friendship is about the complicated enjoyment of human autonomy. As soon as a friend attempts to control a friend, the friendship ceases to exist. But until a lover seeks to possess his beloved, the love has hardly begun. Where love is all about the juggling of the power to hurt, friendship is about creating a space where power ceases to exist. There is a cost to this, of course. Friends will never provide what lovers provide: that ultimate resort, that safe space of repose, that relaxation of the bedsheets. But they provide something more reliable, and certainly less painful. They provide an acknowledgment not of the child within but of the adult without; they allow for an honesty which doesn't threaten pain and a criticism which doesn't imply rejection. They promise not the bliss of the womb but the bracing adventure of the world. They do not solve loneliness, yet they mitigate it.

Ancient writers puzzled over this, because it seemed strange that such a natural relationship should not be based on some sort of vital human need. But if friendship fulfilled some kind of need, it would not, they figured, be truly virtuous. It could be reduced to the same level as the need to eat or drink or have sex (or fall in love). A truly virtuous man, after all, would not need friends. He would be perfect in himself. And yet a truly virtuous man would be surrounded by friends, and some of them would surely be as virtuous as he. How to solve this paradox? A virtuous man, they concluded, would *choose* friends out of sheer pleasure, out of a superfluous desire to communicate and exchange ideas and do good for others, because without them, his very virtue would be denied a platform and an opportunity to flourish. So he comes to a friend in exactly the opposite way that a lover comes to his beloved. He comes not out of need, or passion, or longing. He comes out of a radical choice. Friendship, in this way, is a symbol of man's ultimate freedom from his emotional needs; love is a symbol of his slavery to them.

In modern times, Emerson expressed this most eloquently. For Emerson, friendship was not about losing oneself in another, it was about being more fully oneself:

> The soul environs itself with friends, that it may enter into a grander self-acquaintance or solitude . . . A friend, therefore, is a sort of paradox in nature. I who alone am, I who see nothing in nature whose existence I can affirm with equal evidence to my own, behold now the semblance of my being, in all its height, variety, and curiosity, reiterated in a foreign form; so that a friend may well be reckoned the masterpiece of nature . . . Guard him as thy counterpart. Let him be to thee for ever a sort of beautiful enemy, untamable, devoutly revered . . .

How unlike love, with its pressing, urgent desire for union, for self-oblivion in another's arms. If in a lover we seek an end to our individuation, in a friend we seek its full development. In fact, if union occurs, the very principle of friendship is violated, which is that it be between two radically separate beings. Let your friend, Emerson inveighs,

> not cease an instant to be himself. The only joy I have in his being mine, is that the not mine is

mine. I hate, where I looked for a manly further-
ance, or at least a manly resistance, to find a mush
of concession. Better be a nettle in the side of your
friend than his echo. The condition which high
friendship demands is ability to do without it. That
high office requires great and sublime parts. There
must be very two, before there can be very one. Let
it be an alliance of two large, formidable natures,
mutually beheld, mutually feared, before yet they
recognize the deep identity which beneath these
disparities unites them.

That particular phrase captures it: the "ability to do
without it." How many of us can say that about love in
its highest form, a love that elevates us like a narcotic
and addicts us to its redemptive power? But friendship is
for those who do not want to be saved, for those whose
appreciation of life is here and now and whose comfort in
themselves is sufficient for them to want merely to share
rather than to lose their identity. And they enter into
friendship as an act of radical choice. Friendship, in this
sense, is the performance art of freedom.

And like most truly free things, it does not conform to
any simple purpose or direction. To ask what a friend is
for is to mistake the nature of a friend. A friend is for herself and nothing else. If you enter a friendship to be less
lonely, then it is not a friendship; if you enter it to find
out something, then you are fooling yourself; if you enter
it for profit or even the chance to meet others, then you
have no understanding of it. Love solves a need, answers a
calling, scratches an itch. Friendship does none of these

things. It merely flourishes, a sign that human beings can choose one another for company, enjoy each other's selves, and accompany each other on an enterprise, with no thought of gain or purpose. In a utilitarian world, it is useless in the best sense of the word. It resists the meaning of anything but itself. Friends, as Michael Oakeshott expressed it,

> are not concerned with what might be made of one another, but only with the enjoyment of one another; and the condition of this enjoyment is a ready acceptance of what is and the absence of any desire to change or to improve. A friend is not somebody one trusts to behave in a certain manner, who supplies certain wants, who has certain agreeable qualities, or who holds acceptable opinions; he is somebody who engages the imagination, who excites contemplation, who provokes interest, sympathy, delight and loyalty simply on account of the relationship entered into. One friend cannot replace another; there is all the difference in the world between the death of a friend and the retirement of one's tailor from business. The relationship of friend to friend is dramatic, not utilitarian; the tie is one of familiarity, not usefulness.

Does this imply that friends cannot be of use to one another? Obviously not. Friends are often the most reliable of people in a crisis, and are naturally the first to respond to an emergency or an illness. But if friendship is premised on the need for someone in a pinch, then it is not truly friendship. Indeed, a friend will be reluctant to put his friend on the spot in this way, in case the relationship slips too easily into a mutual fulfillment of needs. That is why a friend will only rarely ask a friend for money, or for lodging, or for a favor. He will not want to strain the relationship with the to-and-fro of purpose and need and direction. In primitive societies, of course, this is what friendship is all about. And even today some believe that they are most a friend when they are taking care of a friend, or when they are fixing some favor, or arranging some introduction. But this is when they are least a friend. When someone is in someone's care or someone's employ, he is incapable of friendship; he is reduced to being a recipient of mere love, unable to achieve the equality and independence which alone make friendship possible. This is why a true friend is relieved when a friend no longer has to stay in his house, or owes him money, or is beset by sickness. For then the friendship can begin again, differentiated from need-love and need-power, liberated to breathe the oxygen of independence.

Because of this independence, a friend can be far more honest than a lover. When a lover is asked for the truth, she has to consider how such a revelation might adversely affect her relationship; and since she needs her lover and her lover needs her, she is under intense pressure to shade her meaning, veil her words, or even, simply, lie. She might do this out of selfishness or even out of concern for her lover (although in a love relationship this is always also a form of selfishness). But a friend is less constrained. She is almost required to tell the truth, because her role is not primarily to support a friend's needs but to accom-

pany a friend's life. And since, in the best form of friendship, she is able to do without the friend, and indeed
premises the friendship on her ultimate independence,
she has far less at stake in risking candor. The loss of a
friend is less immediately painful than losing a lover, and
the loneliness that follows, though considerable, is less
viscerally unbearable.

This is why you can tell a friend things that you can't tell
a lover. You can talk about temptation, and disillusion-
ment, and boredom in your relationship which, if you
brought up in bed, might be too much for the relationship
to bear. We are told constantly how happy marriages and
successful love affairs are built on complete honesty, but
this is obviously bad advice. All love requires something
of an illusion about the other person, because very few
people can objectively merit our complete self-giving, and
illusions require a certain care that they not be discred-
ited. People's pride is involved, and their dreams. Friendships, in contrast, have enough space that bracing honesty
can be a tonic, if applied judiciously. They are places where
the trust is so great, and the distance sufficient, that nothing is out of bounds for discussion, even the most intimate
secrets and humiliating truths. For in love, humiliation is
a real and constant threat; in a true friendship, humiliation is an impossibility.

This, perhaps, is what Jesus meant, in one of the few
moments when he came to talk of friendship, rather than
simply live it. In John's Gospel, he says, "I shall not call
you servants anymore, because a servant does not know
his master's business; I call you friends because I have
made known to you everything I have learnt from my

Father." It is when his relationship with his disciples becomes transparent, when there are no secrets anymore, that he transforms them from servants to friends. This is a silent and sometimes overlooked narrative of John's Gospel. It is the story of love's transformation into friendship. The condition of that friendship is honesty. And it is only when such friends have finally appeared, when such honesty has finally been achieved, that Jesus is able to face the ordeal which almost immediately engulfs him.

WHAT DO WE TELL our friends? We tell them everything. And we are not afraid of embarrassing ourselves or boring each other. After Patrick and I found ourselves in the same viral miasma, there were times when we could tell each other things I don't think we could have told anyone else. I remember lying down on Pat's bed one afternoon, when he was in the middle of the worst infection he had yet had, a brutal little intestinal parasite called microsporidium. This vicious piece of invisible biology had slowly taken over Pat's bowels and made it impossible for him to absorb any food. So he was slowly starving, when he wasn't vomiting and shitting himself. Day by day, he would go through fevers in the low 100s, and night by night, he would lie awake, drenched in sweat, unable to be fully awake, and shaken by fevers out of what passed for sleep. For the first time, I remember, he got that AIDS skull look; for the first time, the sick days began to outnumber the well days; until in those winter months of "micro," we began to contemplate the thing we had not yet been able to contemplate. And as we lay there on the bed, him under the covers, me on top of them, I asked him what he thought death actually was. He was shivering again, and we spooned, that candlewick bedspread holding our bodies inches apart. I remember feeling his bones beneath it for the first time, the skeleton beginning to shape the once firm, rosy flesh of his body.

"I don't know," he said. "I don't really know. Sometimes it seems like some blackness coming toward me. And sometimes, it doesn't seem like anything." He paused, and I felt unqualified to add anything. So we lay there for a while in silence, staring at the ceiling, me wondering if I'd asked him because I was actually curious as to what a dying man might actually think, as if he might know a little better and help me navigate what I thought was ahead of me; or whether I asked him because somebody needed to, and no one else would dare; or, since I was his only close friend facing the same prospect, no one else could ask him. He shivered again, and the phone rang. But death became one more of those banalities we had in common.

Pat was a great writer. One of my favorite letters is one he wrote me while I was away on the Cape. It was an account of a dreary day in his life, while the illness closed in. Waking up, after a terrible night's sleep, was a particular ordeal:

> Then day breaks and the sunlight in the crack of the curtain forces my eyes to respond, and I cover my head with the pillow but soon find the pillow blocks free flow of air and I grow annoyed at the feel of the warm stagnant air I breathe beneath the pillow, so I

try to shape it, squish it down to cover my eyes but not my nose and mouth. This works for a while, but then I want to change positions, perhaps lie on my side, but the prospect of having to negotiate the pillow keeps me frozen in the same position until I finally throw it off and decide in irritation to go ahead and get up.

Patrick noticed the little things, and he passed them along to his friends. He became obsessed with the notion that he was going to lose his senses, especially his sense of smell, which made the world real for him and made food one of life's deepest pleasures. "The other day," he wrote, "I was using ammonia to clean something, and only after I had spent some time with my head close to the basin where the milky ammonia-and-water mixture sat did I realize that the sensation of burning in my eyes was difficult to register as being related to the ammonia without the accompanying olfactory jolt. I put my face closer to the liquid and inhaled through my nose as deeply as I could . . . Nothing. Nada. Not a trace of the smell. Just a burning in my eyes."

These small details were practice runs, it turned out. In the late summer of 1995, Pat was told he had to have a catheter implanted into his chest to deliver permanent doses of antibiotics to keep his infections at bay. For Patrick, it was clearly a sign of capitulation to the virus, a boundary he hated to cross. He delayed the operation until after our annual trip to his hometown to celebrate his birthday. And a few days before we went, he took three of us out to dinner and told us he had decided what he wanted to do with his ashes. His lover and ex-lover told him not to be so gloomy. It was too early and too gruesome to talk about these things. But Pat persisted. There was a spot in the sea near his childhood home, he said, a dark, swiftly deepening shallow off the point where the Gulf of Mexico meets the bay, a place where he used to dive as a child. Rumor has it that sharks lurk there, and as a boy he had dared them to catch him as he plunged into the depths. It was a place his father and grandfather had known; it was where his young nephews and nieces now swam. You could see it from the modest beach house his family owned off the main road clinging to the shore. And it was where, finally, he felt at home. It was classic Pat: a place of refuge and a place of escape, a darkness that led homeward, a wild and tame place, and his.

Later that night he called me again. He was worried his lover and ex-lover were not taking him seriously, or didn't realize how important this was to him. "*You* understand, don't you?" he said on the phone in the dark. I was not too close to find the thought of his death unthinkable, but not too far away to forget what he had told me. Yes, I said. I understood. And I would make sure it happened. Promise. And something in the way he talked to me that night made me realize he thought it was a matter of urgency.

Within days, we were there, pulling up to Sharks' Hole in Patrick's brother's boat. We jumped in and swam, Patrick smiling above the watermark, his freckles covered in salty rivulets. And after a while in the warm, black water, we walked along the shoreline, taking in the place, watching each other watch each other, picking up seashells, and traipsing our feet in the powdery white sand. Nothing remarkable happened, except for one odd thing. A little way ahead of us on the beach, a wounded seagull lay, flapping its wings in distress, making desperate little scratch marks in the sand. As we got closer we saw what was wrong. A small fish had gotten stuck in its craw. Out of its beak, the head of the fish and the tail stuck out together side by side, the fish's body bent double inside the bird's gullet, causing the gull to choke and panic. A small trail of blood ran down its neck as Pat's brother, Dusty, held it down with a piece of driftwood and Pat tugged gently at the fish's tail, tugging again and again, with increasing force, until the fish was finally disgorged, and the gull, bewildered and liberated, flew away, low over the ocean.

FOR THE ANCIENT AND medieval thinkers, friendship was a supreme virtue but it was not everything. Although friendship promised a happiness beyond all happinesses, and a sweetness beyond all sweetnesses, it ceded at some point to a higher principle and found its ultimate meaning beyond itself. For Cicero and Aristotle, that principle was human virtue; for the greatest medieval writer on friendship, a twelfth-century English monk called Aelred of Rievaulx, the principle was the love of Christ. Friendship was one of the highest human goods, but it could never be embraced for its own sake, without disturbing the order of the universe that made it possible. This, again, differentiated it from *eros,* a passion that easily usurped the reason that alone kept virtue within grasp.

Cicero makes this point almost before he makes any other. "All that I can do is to urge you to put friendship before all things human," he tells his interlocutors. "For nothing is so in tune with our nature and nothing so adaptable to our fortune, whether it is good or bad. But this I feel first of all—that friendship cannot exist except among good men." By this, of course, he does not mean the friendships of convenience, mutual advantage, or pleasure, that Aristotle showed such tolerance for. He means the kind of friendship that ascends to the ideal type, between two equals in virtue and sensibility. For it takes a great deal of virtue to sustain the discipline of the highest friendship, to be capable of the complete trust, stability, maturity, and concern for the good that a real friend must possess. So a true friend will never put his friend in a moral dilemma; he will not ask him to do what is wrong, or ask him to place their friendship before the common good, or demand that he lie for him, or make excuses for him.

Cicero wonders whether a true friend of Themistocles or Coriolanus could have supported them even when they rebelled against their own countries. And his answer is unequivocal: "Alliance of wicked men not only shouldn't be protected by a plea of friendship, but rather they should be visited with summary punishment of the severest kind, so that no one may think it permissible to follow even a friend when waging war against his own country." One is reminded of E. M. Forster's famous remark that if he were forced to choose between his friends and his country, he hoped he would have the courage to choose his friends. Aristotle would have found the remark nonsensical;

Cicero would have found it contemptible. And one is reminded of the apocryphal but brilliant scene in Robert Bolt's play about Thomas More, *A Man for All Seasons*. At one point, one of More's oldest friends, the Duke of Norfolk, urges More to acquiesce to Henry VIII's divorce "for fellowship's sake." But More found the idea of preferring friendship to what he regarded as a moral and political principle to be corrosive of friendship itself. For would a true friend want his friend to betray himself? Although there's no doubting Norfolk's sincerity in his attempt to save More from the consequences of his obstinacy, he is flouting what Cicero would regard as the rules of *amicitia*. And More was a good Ciceronian. He refuses Norfolk's plea with the pointed, devastating question: "And when we stand before God, and you are sent to Paradise for doing according to your conscience, and I am damned for not doing according to mine, will you come with me, for fellowship?"

Such a conviction about the essential congruity between virtue and friendship was central to the work of Aelred of Rievaulx. For Aelred, true friendship seems at times a kind of mystical delirium, an essential step toward knowledge of and acquiescence to God's love. For Aelred, "nothing more sacred is striven for, nothing more useful is sought after, nothing more difficult is discovered, nothing more sweet experienced, and nothing more profitable possessed." Reading him is to be aware of a world where asexual and unromantic friendship nevertheless reaches an intensity that can only be called ecstatic. He describes the union of friendship as a kind of "spiritual kiss":

> For [friendship] is not made by contact of the mouth
> but by the affection of the heart; not by a meeting of
> the lips but by a mingling of the spirits, by the purifi-
> cation of all things in the Spirit of God, and, through
> his own participation, it emits a celestial savor. I
> would call this the kiss of Christ, yet he himself does
> not offer it from his own mouth, but from the mouth
> of another, breathing upon his lovers that most
> sacred affection so that there seems to be, as it were,
> one spirit in many bodies . . . The soul, therefore,
> accustomed to this kiss and not doubting that all
> this sweetness comes from Christ, as if reflecting
> within itself and saying, "Oh, if only he himself had
> come!" sighs for the kiss of grace and with the great-
> est desire exclaims: "Let him kiss me with the kiss of
> his mouth!"

It would be easy to see this as a form of erotic sublimation—from a celibate monk at that. But that, I think,
would be to condescend to Aelred's spiritual sincerity. For
Aelred, the spiritual union is, indeed, like an erotic union
in its bliss, but not sexual in the corporeal sense. He
expresses the old truth about spiritual ecstasy—that such
ecstasy is not a sublimation of sex, but rather that sex
is an intimation of such ecstasy. And such ecstasy,
by definition, cannot obliterate the demands of virtue,
since it is impossible without it: "For what more sublime can be said of friendship, what more true, what more
profitable, than that it ought to, and is proved to, begin in
Christ, continue in Christ, and be perfected in Christ?" He
goes on:

For it is difficult, no, impossible, for you to taste the beginnings of friendship, if you do not know the fountain from which it can spring. For that love is shameful and unworthy of the name of friendship wherein anything foul is demanded of a friend; and this is precisely what one is forced to do, if, with vices in no wise dormant or subdued, he is either enticed or impelled to all sorts of evil acts. So we should detest the opinion of those who think that one should act in behalf of a friend in a way detrimental to faith and uprightness. For it is no excuse for sin, that you sin for the sake of a friend.

This, of course, is a demanding standard, perhaps too demanding. Most friendships, after all, do not rise to the level of complete virtue. They require a constant capacity for forgiveness and flexibility, and the complicity of friends in each other's faults need not amount to a capitulation to evil. Both Aelred and Cicero concede this at other times. They understand that, even in the best of friends, there will be many moments of failure, even vice, and although a good friend will not want to encourage a friend in such weakness, he will inevitably tolerate it at times, listen to it, even provide a form of human solidarity with it. Sometimes, Cicero confides, a friend will go astray, but loyalty demands that we stick with him, "provided . . . utter disgrace does not follow." There is in these thinkers both an uncompromising belief in the regulation of friendship by virtue, and yet a practical sense that friendship can endure, even when virtue doesn't. Nobody's perfect, after all.

But this leads to a paradox. How can one completely trust another imperfect human being, whose faults are all too obvious and who could therefore betray you at any time? The truth is, you can't, and yet without that trust, true friendship itself is impossible. This is why, for Aelred, friendship is such a rare but beautiful thing, and why the betrayal of confidences is such a profound vice, since it undermines the very basis of friendship's possibility. The betrayal of a friend is thus more invidious and more wounding than the betrayal of a lover, since the honesty of a friend is deeper than that of a lover, and the secrets betrayed more profound. And while we might rush foolishly into love, heedless of a lover's character, a friend-turned-enemy reflects very badly on our own judgment. If a friend abandons us, the friendship should therefore be unraveled very delicately, in proportion to the friend's degeneracy. If he turns virulently hostile, then you have little option but to bear his insults with equanimity. On no account, Aelred advises, should you fight back, "for it is most shameful to wage a war of this kind with a man with whom you have lived on terms of intimacy."

The only security against this kind of betrayal is the virtue of Christ, just as, for Cicero, the only guarantee against it was the prudential judgment of the virtuous citizen, and the network of culture and education which made such civic friendship graspable. How vastly different from the modern world of Montaigne, where friendship contains all the intensity of the ancient world but is cut off from the ancients' moral universe, floating free in the air of modern freedom, unconstrained by the

Christian faith that Aelred saw as central to the relationship. The essay "On Friendship," written in honor of Montaigne's dead friend, Étienne de la Boétie, marks, perhaps, a landmark in the emergence of the Western individual. For in it, Montaigne poses an almost enrapturing notion of what friendship is and yet suggests that as soon as it is available, it may be impossible.

The essay hardly mentions virtue. The relationship of two souls is, for Montaigne, superior to such concerns. It is, in a manner of speaking, beyond good and evil. "Our friendship has no other model but itself," Montaigne declaims, "and can be compared only with itself." He later asserts, remarkably, that "a single dominant friendship dissolves all other obligations." By this, he certainly means, echoing Forster, that friendship trumps loyalty to one's country and, even more certainly, loyalty to one's family. Montaigne is scorching about the dreadful obligations of marriage, and brutal about the randomness of family ties. Why, he wonders, should one feel love for someone with whom one shares the accident of emerging from the same womb? He gleefully cites Aristippus, who, "when pressed about the affection he owed his children for having come out of him, he began to spit, saying that that had come out of him just as well, and that we also bred lice and worms." Montaigne's language is designed to shock, but his point is well taken. The essential fact about family is that it is unchosen, and because it is unchosen, it does not belong in the same category of moral freedom and excellence as friendship. It inspires duty, but it certainly doesn't evoke a moral claim.

How odd this sounds to modern ears. We have so thoroughly forgotten the moral claims of freedom that we instinctively ascribe a higher morality to familial love than to friendship. Even when we praise our friends, we are accustomed to saying, "They are like a family to me." But for Montaigne, that is an insult to friendship, and a grotesque misunderstanding of the relationship. In Montaigne's world, indeed in any world which holds freedom dear, it would be better to praise one's family as approximating the virtues of friendship than the other way around. And those loves which are most instinctual and most overpowering, like a mother's love for a child, are the most suspect on these grounds. However beautiful and profound, they are essentially inferior to the sublime nobility of a love based on a free and radical choice.

And for Montaigne, friendship is certainly superior to erotic love, which he icily dismisses as an "attempt to form a friendship inspired by beauty." In perhaps the perfect literary expression of the difference between these two experiences, Montaigne writes that the ardor of *eros* is undoubtedly

> more active, more scorching, and more intense. But it is an impetuous and fickle flame, undulating and variable, a fever flame, subject to fits and lulls, that holds us only in one corner. In friendship it is a general and universal warmth, all gentleness and smoothness, with nothing bitter and stinging about it . . . Thus these two passions within me came to be known to each other, but to be compared, never; the first,

friendship, keeping its course in proud and lofty flight, and disdainfully watching the other make its way far, far beneath it.

But the friendship which Montaigne describes is a peculiarly passionate one. There is none of Emerson's separateness, and much that resonates with Romantic self-renunciation. Indeed, at times, in this case, it is hard to avoid the conclusion that Montaigne was in love with his friend, but felt impelled by the constraints of the time to disguise it. How else can one interpret the following:

> In the friendship I speak of, our souls mingle and blend with each other so completely they efface the seam that joined them, and cannot find it again . . . It is not one special consideration, nor two, nor three, nor four, nor a thousand: it is I know not what quintessence of all this mixture, which, having seized his whole will, led it to plunge and lose itself in mine, with equal hunger, equal rivalry. I say lose, in truth, for neither of us reserved anything for himself, nor was anything either his or mine.

Except, of course, that Montaigne is quite clear that he had no physical attraction to La Boétie and didn't consummate his friendship sexually. It existed rather as a platonic longing so intense that we have almost forgotten how to achieve it today. It is a form of union which is truer than love, stabler than sex, deeper than politics, and more moral than family. And it is perhaps the very uniqueness of this form of union with another being that is the source of Montaigne's enthusiasm. For friendship, for Montaigne, seems to be the final and only answer to the modern dilemma of loneliness. Today, we seek to expunge that loneliness by an endless succession of distractions, by an amnesiac popular culture, by the anesthetic of material wealth, by the chimera of romantic love, or the comfort and proximity of family. Not so long ago, theorists posited a political solution to this alienation—a surrender to the total ideology of the state. But Montaigne held out an alternative to these palliatives. And it was *l'amitié*.

Where is God in this? Or moral virtue? Good questions. You can peer long and hard into Montaigne's prose to find anything but lip service to the idea of such moral authority. Instead, what seems to unite Montaigne and La Boétie, as Allan Bloom has argued, is the same intellectual quest, a tiny island of philosophic unity that makes the world far less lonely for those able to think for themselves—together. In this, Montaigne reflects Plato's implication in the *Lysis* that friendship is perhaps indefinable except in the practice of two or more people trying to define it. It is almost as if a pure union cannot be achieved through bodily contact, or even through a harmony of two sensibilities. Only through the abstract form of ideas can a true fellowship be achieved, and even that, perhaps, for only a while.

And in this, Montaigne represents a radical break from his predecessors. We never quite know the content of the ideas that united him and La Boétie, and Montaigne balks at providing evidence of his friend's serious work (he serves us up a bunch of inane poems instead). But what

Montaigne implies by this is that the actual ideas are irrelevant. What matters is the joint pursuit of them—even to scandalous ends, even in search of answers that bear no relationship to the perfect ordering of Aelred's Christianity or Cicero's civic virtue. From now on, friendship is unmoored from its moral harbor. The relationship premised on freedom has become free itself, free to flout convention and even law, free to do what we have come to think only love can do, free even to defy the attempt to impose meaning upon it. As Montaigne famously put it, "If you press me to tell why I loved him, I feel that this cannot be expressed, except by answering: Because it was he, because it was I." Is it any wonder that this sublime friendship lasted only a tiny amount of time before death interrupted it? And that Montaigne could say of such a union that it was unlikely to happen more than once every three hundred years?

TO MY OTHER FRIENDS who insist that I was in love with Patrick, I can only insist that our relationship was no less intense for being friendship. Montaigne, I felt, would have understood. And sometimes, in my more meandering moments, I wonder whether such friendship would have been so accessible to us if we had not been homosexual. I'm not saying, of course, that friendship is unique to homosexuals. Far from it. But the trajectory of a homosexual life often places, in a way unique to itself, a focus on friendship that many heterosexuals, to their great loss, never quite attain. In fact, I think the primary distinction between homosexuals and heterosexuals in our society is not that they are attracted to different genders, and certainly not that their sexual lives and needs are radically different from each other. It is that homosexuals, by default as much as anything else, have managed to sustain a society of friendship that is, for the most part, unequaled by almost any other part of the society. Heterosexual women have long sustained it, of course, when their familial responsibilities have not overwhelmed them. But heterosexual men, to their great spiritual and emotional impoverishment, have for far too long let it pass them by.

It is astonishing, perhaps, that this is not observed more often. One typical writer has characterized gay culture as a "culture of desire." But this is condescending exaggeration. Desire suffuses gay and straight life, and it no more drives gay men than it does straight men. Indeed, the obsession with sexualizing gay men—an obsession driven by gay radicals as much as by straight conservatives—is a function of the erotocentrism and decadent Christianity that distort so much of modern, particularly American, life. What gay culture really is before it is anything else, before it is a culture of desire or a culture of subversion or a culture of pain, is a culture of friendship.

And I think this begins early in a homosexual life. Friendship, in homosexual development, plays a pivotal part not just in socialization, but in the emergence of identity itself. For a gay child or adolescent doesn't really have a friend in the true sense of the term until he has a friend who knows and accepts the fact that he is gay. When he finds this friend, who is almost always gay himself, the relationship has a significance often far deeper than the first friend a heterosexual child discovers. Because, in a way, it is only when the gay child finds this first true friend that he can really exist at all. Until then, only a part of him exists, the public part, the part that has learned how to act and portray a real person, while the essential person, in his deepest self, remains hidden from view, even, in many cases, from himself and almost always from the people he cares about most, his family.

So the first true friendship, for the homosexual child, is often a revelation. It is simultaneous with the establishment of identity. Whereas most heterosexual children become themselves most transparently in the context of their family, gay children, more often than not, only truly become themselves in the context of their first, true friends. I remember a poem I wrote as a teenager, as excruciating as most such adolescent poems are. But it ended with an astringent observation. "I'm a professional human being," I wrote. "But what do I do in my private life?" It was only when I found my friends that I had a private life at all.

This cultural polarization between family-based heterosexuals and friend-based homosexuals is, of course, unfortunate. It distorts both gay and straight lives and creates unnecessary pain and loneliness for all of us. Perhaps the most important cultural aim of the modern homosexual movement, then, should be to bring the homosexual child back into the fold of his or her family, or, rather, to allow the family to be the emotional bedrock of every child's life, gay and straight. This should not be at the expense of friendship, of course. It should be friendship's emotional complement. And if one were to devise a parallel social aim for a putative heterosexual movement, it would surely be the opposite. It would be to open the heterosexual life—especially the male heterosexual life—to the possibilities of intimacy and support that friendship offers, to vent the family with the fresh air of friendship, to expand the range of relationships and connections that every heterosexual person can achieve.

Oddly enough, I think you see this happening already. You see the gay movement abandoning its radical roots to reconcile gay men and women with their families and communities as a whole. And you see networks of heterosexual women finding new strength and self-confidence in a world where marriages are later, divorce is more common, and long periods of life are lived outside of the marital bond. You see it in the Men's Movement and even in the phenomena of Promise Keepers or the Million Man March. All these are fledgling attempts to forge some kind of social belonging among men that provides greater support than the etiolated and awkward gestures of the 1950s. You see it in the extraordinary depiction of friendship in popular culture, from the most popular sitcoms of the day, *Friends* and *Seinfeld,* to the most popular dramas, such as *E.R.,* which subliminally celebrates the professional bonds of strangers. You see it in hugely popular books such as *Girlfriends* and unexpectedly successful movies such as *Waiting to Exhale* or *My Best Friend's Wedding.* In all this, the need for nonfamilial and nonsexual intimacy is surely uppermost in our minds, however hard it is for us to articulate it.

The end of this century, we are told, has been about the

reconstitution of the family. But the corollary of this, surely, is that it is also about the revival of friendship as a social institution. From the flourishing chat rooms on the Internet to friendship-friendly e-mail and to the coffee bars and health clubs that increasingly dominate our bourgeois modes of interaction, networks of friends are increasingly complementing the networks of family. And this can only improve both institutions. Families and marriages fail too often because they are trying to answer too many human needs. A spouse is required to be a lover, a friend, a mother, a father, a soulmate, a co-worker, and so on. Few people can be all these things for one person. And when demands are set too high, disappointment can only follow. If husbands and wives have deeper and stronger friendships outside the marital unit, the marriage has more space to breathe and fewer burdens to bear. Likewise, a lack of true family can, I think, impinge on friendship. If we have many friends and no real family, we tend to demand of friends things which are equally inappropriate—the need-love and deep security that only lovers and parents and spouses can provide. The two relationships, then, family and friendship, are surely rivals, but they are also complements to one another. There is no reason why most human lives should not have a deep experience of both.

And this applies perhaps especially to heterosexual men. The fear of male intimacy, which is intrinsically connected to a fear of homosexuality, has too often denied straight men the bonds they need to sustain themselves through life's difficulties. When they socialize, they too often demand the chaperone of sports or work to avoid the appearance of being gay. Or they need to congregate in groups that tend to diminish the quiet intimacy that all of us need. How often, for example, do two adult straight men go out to dinner together? Or merely spend time doing nothing together? Perhaps the most overlooked benefit of a culture which can relax its strictures against homosexual love and life is that we could finally liberate heterosexual life to experience a more fluid and satisfying and intimate range of nonsexual relations without the fear of stigma or moral panic. This is why the movement for homosexual liberation is actually a misnomer. It is a movement for human liberation, and heterosexuals stand to gain from it as much as anyone.

LEARNING TO ACCEPT a friend can be the hardest part. There were many parts of Patrick that rankled, puzzled me, infuriated me. His elusiveness, his anger, his pride. I know from his journals and his gripes that he felt the same way about me. He thought me often distant and self-obsessed, arrogant and vain. These were not our only differences. Pat was obsessed with food; food bored me. Pat was an elaborate gift giver; if I remembered a birthday, I considered it a monumental achievement. Pat was driven by literature and music; I found my passions in philosophy and history and politics. I was a careerist; Pat was ambivalent about any form of conventional success. Pat hardly ever threw anything away; I rarely kept anything. And given these differences, it would have been possible for us merely to tolerate each other, enjoy each other's company for what it was worth, and leave the rest behind. But, for some reason, we didn't. There is a world of difference between tolerance and acceptance. Tolerance is that distant agreement to live and let live, a political and social virtue as necessary as it is difficult. Acceptance is an impassioned, often hostile, engagement with 90 percent of a person and a complete embrace of all of him. It is a personal and private virtue. And friendship, at its heart, is not about tolerance. Friendship is about acceptance.

I've no doubt that, with Pat and me, this acceptance was fueled in part by our common homosexuality and in part by our common disease. We were in the same battle, not least for ourselves, but also, we believed, for others. Both of us began in mainstream careers—he in Capitol Hill politics, then publishing; me in academia and then political journalism. But both of us also found ourselves, as we grew and strengthened, drawn to what seemed to be the more pressing demand of our time: the political and social and moral struggle for the equality of our kind. So Pat ended up working for an AIDS organization, and I ended up writing and speaking about homosexuality. And we both refused, in very different ways, to abandon our Church. I think we both knew in our hearts that, in this sense, our values were identical. We knew what we believed to be the most obvious challenge to us in the time and place we happened to find ourselves. And we respected each other's determination to confront it. Both of us were also dogged traditionalists, revering ancient writers and classical composers, bored if not amused by academic fashion, skeptical of politics, enraged by the idiocy of much of what passed for gay activism. So we also

shared a similar displacement from the battle we enjoined, and helped each other find a way of living with it.

We came from small towns, and Catholic families, although Patrick was obsessed with his background in a
way I never was with mine. And although Patrick's relationship with his faith was far more elaborate and opaque
than my own, the few times that we knelt together at
Mass, and bowed our heads together at Communion, were
times that are hard to forget. Our mutual friend, Alane,
and the two of us, once went to Mass together in Washington. It was in the last year of Pat's life. We said nothing but
the common words of the liturgy. And after Communion,
we looked up from our prayers to find simple tears in each
other's eyes. There is a lot of rhetoric spoken in today's
Church about the need for "faith-community." But what
we felt was something closer to "faith-friendship": unspoken, left alone, resilient. It kept us going.

And Pat kept me going. During our friendship, I went
through a period of notoriety, and while other friends
withdrew or cast aspersions or grew attracted to the
attention, Patrick remained completely the same. His
attachment to me, I found out, had nothing to do with
anything around me, anything I had written, anything
I had done, or any fame that I had accrued. He was
alternately proud and critical of me, scornful of my occasional stupidity but doggedly supportive of my happiness. I remember one night in particular when Pat and I
went out to a bar together. It was during a period when I
was more than usually in public view, and acquaintance
after acquaintance, and stranger after stranger, treated
me with that odd familiarity that exposure can engender.

Some friends would have resented it; others would have enjoyed it, others still would have found it ridiculous. But Patrick simply said to me, "There they go again. Giving you that 'untouchable' look." Pat had seen only one thing during all that distraction. And that was that it was actually very isolating. And he made it less so.

And it was because of the extraordinary support of his love that the hardest part of accepting Patrick was his refusal to tackle his illness more aggressively. From the beginning, he delayed getting tested and avoided confronting the possibility of his infection. He ducked the issue, as was his custom, rather than dealing with it. And when he finally had no choice but to face it, he took a typically idiosyncratic tack. He was convinced that his only option was to treat the opportunistic infections that successively racked him, rather than to fight HIV directly. He was too far gone, he thought, to adopt any other strategy. When he found out he had AIDS, his T cells were around 50, compared to around 1,000 in most healthy people. The medical handbooks of the time described this condition as late-stage AIDS, and gave him six to eighteen months to live. Pat took this diagnosis as real, and although he did what he could to fight the disease, he never mentally believed he would survive for long, and acted accordingly.

Sometimes I thought he behaved this way because to do otherwise would be to give HIV too much power over him. His irrationality was an expression of his remaining freedom. So when a new drug, 3TC, came on the market, I begged him to use it as part of combination antiviral therapy. But he masterfully dodged my badgering and avoided a

simple and, for many, powerful therapy. He made only fitful attempts to get hold of the new protease inhibitors, the
drugs that saved so many of his peers. And when his doctor
urged him to wear a catheter to keep bacterial infections
at bay, he tempted fate by delaying the insertion of the
catheter until after his birthday celebration in his hometown. I remember a phone conversation with him only
three weeks before he died when I told him I thought he
should put the catheter in right away, because to give the
disease any opening could be a fatal gamble he might lose.
He deflected my arguments. Till the end, he was not going
to cede timing or comfort or freedom to the disease. He was
too proud.

But a prickly pride was also an intrinsic part of Patrick. In
fact, it is hard to conceive of him without it. What would it
mean, I ask myself now, for Patrick to have become not-
Patrick and to have lived, rather than to have remained
Patrick and died? At some point in friendship, you have to
take someone as a whole, and love them for all of it, and
cherish their existence as it is and not as you might want it
to be. So when I miss Pat now, and I miss him terribly, I resist
the temptation to be angry with him for not being here anymore; because, in some ways, the price of his being Patrick
during the time that he lived was that he was unlikely to be
here very long. He was gay and a sexual adventurer. He was
born in the 1960s. The odds of his growing to adulthood,
given who he was, in the era of AIDS, without becoming
HIV-positive, were, I think, close to zero. And the odds of
his taking a rational, humble, one-dimensional medical
approach to his illness while remaining true to himself
were also, I think, close to zero. So the story of Pat was

always going to be, in part, what the story of Pat turned out to be. Or something very close to it. Yes, he had some unlucky breaks. And yes, he wasn't completely proud or completely perverse—that would have given my arguments too much credibility. And yes, he suffered enormously and bravely and tenaciously a series of illnesses that would have broken anyone's spirit. But his spirit was never broken. His spirit was subversive and mischievous and brilliant to the last. And it taunted a disease that eventually killed him. But Patrick himself endured. He was himself to the end. He never compromised his character or his idiosyncrasy or his freedom for a second. This was why, of course, I loved him. Because he was him. In the words of Anatole Broyard, Patrick was alive when he died. How much better than to be dead when he survived.

CAN WE BE FRIENDS with God? This is a question which may seem quaint today, easily dismissed as a televangelist's cute cliché or an ancient theological quarrel. To nonbelievers, it can seem an irrelevant digression, but the echoes of the argument reverberate in contemporary secular debates far removed from medieval obscurities. And it seems to me to be central to any true assessment of friendship's worth. For the oldest and deepest criticism of friendship is not that it isn't *eros* but that it isn't *agape*. By *agape*, I mean what we used to call charity or *caritas*. I mean the love Saint Paul described in his letter to the Corinthians, in his reference to faith, hope, and love. I mean the extraordinary notion that "God is Love," the

Christian and, indeed, Kantian idea of disinterested love, love of our neighbor, love of one's enemies, love of those who hate us, love of those we do not even know, love of those we have not even met. I mean the constant and unresolvable question of loyalty—to whom and to what extent we owe it—a question that is as much political as it is moral, as much modern as it is ancient.

In most Christian discussions of friendship, this rivalry between *amicitia* and *caritas* has emerged as the central issue. If friendship is based on likeness, reciprocity, and equality, then how can it exist between human beings and God? If friendship is inherently reciprocal, then how can it be extended to enemies? And if the love that we are asked to extend indiscriminately to our fellow human beings is rooted in the love of God, then how can it be related to friendship? Indeed, isn't friendship in some ways antithetical to this love, a danger and a threat to it, and a debilitating distraction?

Augustine, unsurprisingly, was there first. The lesson he drew from the grief he felt for his dead friend was not the value of friendship but its deceptiveness. He realized that the more he had invested in this human love, the more vulnerable he was to loss, since his love was for something mortal and finite and fallible. It was therefore a contradiction—something that, in its perfection and equality, suggested eternity, but something that was, in fact, devastatingly temporary. So for Augustine, the end of friendship was the beginning of faith:

> For wherever the human soul turns itself, other than to you, [O God], it is fixed in sorrows, even if it is

fixed upon beautiful things external to you and external to itself, which would nevertheless be nothing if they did not have their being from you. Things rise and set: in their emerging they begin as it were to be, and grow to perfection; having reached perfection, they grow old and die. Not everything grows old, but everything dies. So when things rise and emerge into existence, the faster they grow to be, the quicker they rush towards non-being.

It is to guard against this transience that Augustine learned to cherish *agape* over *philia*. And indeed, it was to become a theological truism that this very distinction was central to the difference between Christianity and paganism. With Christianity, the impermanence of friendship was to be superseded by the eternal security of God's incarnated, universal love. For pagans, friendship was everything, and love for humanity as a whole meaningless and empty. For Christians, although friendship remained a virtue, it was dangerously prone to exclusiveness, to a preference for some over others, and thus a subtle but profound distraction from Christ's injunction to express radical love for all.

Kierkegaard was later to make this case in its most extreme form, excoriating friendship almost as a vice: "Christian love teaches love of all men, unconditionally all," he thundered. "Let the poet search the New Testament for a word about friendship which could please him, and he will search vainly unto despair." Kant too inveighed against what seemed to be the inherent immorality of friendship. He subtly reordered Aristotle's categories of *philia* in chronological order, with friendships of need coming first in human history, followed by friendships of "disposition," and then a universal friendship of morality. In Kant's progressive civilization, friendships of even Montaigne's highest form were slowly evolving to a higher principle, to a purer, universal friendship in which every human being would feel the same regard for every other human being, and friendship, in the partial, personal, exclusive sense, would slowly, mercifully, wither away.

Friendship is clearly threatening to these thinkers, and you can see why. *Amicitia* is a matter of sensibility; *caritas* is a matter of will. *Philia* is human; *agape* is divine. Friendship, even when it is virtuous, is a natural human capacity, but love is always and everywhere a gift from God. Despite friendship's pretension to equality, it is inevitably exclusionary and therefore unequal. So even when friendship is pure, and free, and based on goodwill, it is also solitary, exclusionary, and, by implication, hostile to outsiders. Friendship strengthens with mutual awareness and with time, but love is instant and universal, to be extended to those we do not even like and with whom we have nothing whatsoever in common.

The obvious and natural defense of friendship against this assault is to argue, as Kant did in part, and as Aristotle did instinctively, in defense of friendship's practicability. It is extremely difficult, after all, for human beings to feel universal love, especially for those we do not particularly like. The best that we can practically do, perhaps, is to build on the practice of friendship toward a more general goodwill toward others. Indeed, you might argue, by undermining the practical possibility of friendship, you make it less likely for people to achieve even a modicum of charity for others. Because, in reality, charity takes wing on the shoulders of friendship; without friendship, charity would not know where to begin.

This is an ancient debate, and it certainly isn't over yet. You can even see in it, I think, an early forerunner of the modern, political split between "liberals" and "conservatives." Liberals, in true Augustinian fashion, are suspicious of particular loyalties and seek to embrace universal values and egalitarian politics. Theirs is the politics of *caritas*. Conservatives, in contrast, prefer particulars to universals, and *amicitia* to love. They see more virtue in one person's actual regard for another than in, say, a welfare system which reflects a more consistent but more distant moral order. And they are also more likely to prefer nationalism to internationalism, and to support voluntary over political associations. Theirs is the politics of *philia*.

But just as modern politics finds a natural, if constantly shifting, balance between the political claims of universalism and particularism, so there might seem to be a moral *via media* as well, a plausible path between the Kierkegaardian either-or, one that manages to preserve the virtue of friendship while not denying the moral demands of love. Aquinas presents one possibility, although it is limited, perhaps, to a theological perspective. For Aquinas, although there was an obviously incommensurate difference between God, the fount of charity, and human beings, the practitioners of friendship, there was also a communication between the two. Indeed, insofar as humans were spiritual beings, there was even what he called a "conversation" between them and the angels, and between them and God. And the basis for that conversation had to be the basis for any conversation, which was some sort of friendship.

It was, perhaps, similar to the friendship Aristotle observed between two radically unequal partners, a friendship in which equality was reached but only by each recognizing the unequal nature of their relative positions. And for both parties, recognizing the rules of friendship, the communication was completely voluntary. God, of course, has no need as such of communicating to man; and man, given free will, is allowed to choose to communicate with God or not. And so something like *philia* emerges: "Since there is a communication between man and God, inasmuch as he communicates His happiness to us," Aquinas reasons, "some kind of friendship must needs be based on this same communication . . . The love which is based on this communication, is charity: wherefore it is evident that charity is the friendship of man for God."

"Charity is the friendship of man for God." The more you think about this idea, the more extraordinary it is. What it suggests is not the superior morality of love to friendship, but the opposite: the radical notion that love is only fully realized in friendship. Love, Aquinas argues, is man's friendship for God. Just as we cannot know God, we cannot know our neighbor. So we love our neighbor as we have learnt to love God—as a friend. The key to achieving charity, in other words, is to approximate the friendship that we feel for God and to extend it to others. Isn't this, after all, what Jesus enjoined: to see him in every person, to remember that whatever we do for the least of his brethren, we do for him? And isn't this just another way of saying that if there is a relationship of friendship between God and man, then this must be the definition of charity between human beings?

When we die, of course, we will actually know God, and the friendship that we will have for him will not be premised on unknowing, but on seeing face to face. It will be love-become-friendship. So too, presumably, will be our knowledge of each other after death. Charity, then, is not the antithesis of friendship. It is the universalization of friendship, a universalization that is impossible on earth, except by divine intervention, but exquisitely, overpoweringly, present after death. This, perhaps, is what Heaven truly is: it is when our love of God becomes friendship with him, and true friendship with each other, because it is only then that we finally know him, and true transparency can begin. "I shall not call you servants anymore, because a servant does not know his master's business; I call you friends because I have made known to you everything I have learnt from my Father."

This was Aelred's answer to the conundrum as well. The key to friendship, he seems to say, is intimacy. Intimacy on earth cannot be universal, simply because in time and space, we cannot know everyone. So human friendship is *agape* plus intimacy. So it is not a competitor with love; it is, in fact, the fullest realization of love. It is love with knowledge. As Aelred said of his dead friend, "There was no pretense between us, no simulation, no dishonorable flattery, no unbecoming harshness, no evasion, no concealment, but everything open and above board; for I deemed my heart in a fashion his, and his mine, and he felt in like manner toward me." How could any love for a stranger be deeper or greater than this?

Think again of Jesus' famous words in John's Gospel: "No greater love has a man than this: that he lay down his life for his friends." How many times have we heard that phrase? And how many times have we glided over its most important word? "No greater love has a man than this: that he lay down his life for his *friends*." He does not say, "No greater love has a man than this: that he lay down his life for humanity." No, the love of those we know is inherently deeper and greater than our love for those we do not know. And the impossible goal of the moral life on earth is to feel that kind of love for strangers. Indeed, love is only fully manifest when it is expressed through the medium of friendship.

It is strange that this requires elaboration, since it is a message scattered throughout the Gospels. Jesus went to many places, he embraced strangers and foreigners, the outcast and the lonely. He fully expressed the importance of charity to others. But he was also, first and foremost, a friend. He didn't live in a family—indeed he was a cause of great pain to his natural family. He chose to live in a group of twelve men and a handful of women, with whom he was clearly and deeply emotionally involved. There are so many stories of his friendships in the Gospels, but we have learned, the way we learn elsewhere in our culture, to glide over them, or to see in them a message about something else other than the relationship they illustrate. What, after all, is the meaning of his famous injunction to Martha that her sister, Mary, has chosen the "one thing necessary," when all that Mary is doing is sitting at Jesus' feet and being with her friend? What else could the meaning be of Jesus' primary commandment to "love one another" if it doesn't mean to love one's friends? He gave that order, after all, not to a crowd of strangers but to the group of friends who are known to us as the apostles. "You are my friends," he said, "if you do what I command you." And what he commanded, indeed the primary thing he commanded, was to love one another. As friends.

But perhaps few such stories are as revealing as his resurrection of Lazarus. We have gotten so used to this story, to its redemptive prefiguring of Jesus' own emergence from death, that we tend to forget who Lazarus actually was. Lazarus was Jesus' friend. He was the brother of Martha and Mary, the women whom Jesus, we are told, would peremptorily drop in on without warning, the women who, as much as anyone, appear in the Gospels as Jesus' close friends. So Jesus was moved to the most radical act of his ministry by grief and love for a dead friend and for his living sisters.

The story begins with an odd detail. Although Jesus knew that Lazarus was sick, for some reason he didn't rush to his bedside. Both Martha and Mary reprimand him for this, coming out of Bethany to reproach him bitterly for his irresponsibility. They make an astonishing accusation, each telling Jesus in grief and anger, "If you had been here, my brother would not have died." In essence, they blame Jesus for their brother's death. At this, we are told, Jesus "said in great distress, with a sigh that came straight from the heart, 'Where have you put him?' They said, 'Lord, come and see.' Jesus wept; and the Jews said, 'See how much he loved him.'" Jesus must surely know, we are invited to understand, that what he is about to do will transform his life. So far in his ministry, he has only performed minor miracles, cures of blindness and leprosy, multiplication of loaves and fishes, but to raise someone from the dead will surely turn him into a sensation and hasten the building resentment of his rivals and the moment of his death. So he wrestles with his fear for the future and his love for his friends. The sigh comes straight from his heart. And he performs the miracle of all miracles. And he performs it for friendship's sake.

The evangelist who tells us this story is John, the disciple, we are told, whom Jesus loved. This love of Jesus for one particular man, who fully and uniquely reciprocated, is the other striking indication of how vital friendship was in Jesus' life and teaching. It suggests how even the preacher of *agape* was in fact a practitioner of *philia*, and a devoted one at that. John was not the supreme disciple. The responsibility for the Church was bestowed, after all, on Peter. But John was clearly the disciple with whom Jesus was most intimate. If Jesus gave Peter the Church, to John Jesus entrusted his mother, and at the moment of his death, as his last act as a human being. John was the only disciple to stay with Jesus at the moment of his death. And he was the first disciple to arrive at the empty tomb, running ahead of Peter, as if seized with a greater urgency and need to know what had happened to his crucified friend.

With John, Jesus' intimacy was, at times, of a physical intensity. Aelred remembers the Last Supper, when only John was able to ask Jesus the terrifyingly intimate question of who it is who will betray him. Peter doesn't dare, and merely jogs John to ask the Master. And in order to ask the question, we are told that John rested his head on Jesus' breast. "Who is it, Lord?" he ventured. "To Peter," Aelred notices, "he gave the keys of his kingdom; to John, he revealed the secrets of his heart. Peter, therefore, was the more exalted; John, the more secure . . . Peter was exposed to action, John was reserved for love."

And this delicate competition between these two disciples continues to the very end of the Gospels, even to the days when Jesus walked the earth as a resurrected figure. On the shore of Tiberias, Jesus asks Peter not once but three times, "Do you love me more than these others do? . . . Do you love me? . . . Do you love me?" And after each of Peter's protestations that he did indeed love him, Jesus orders him to take care of his sheep. After this, he tells Peter to follow him.

And then something strange happens:

> Peter turned and saw the disciple Jesus loved following them—the one who had leaned on his breast at the supper and had said to him, "Lord, who is it that will betray you?" Seeing him, Peter said to Jesus, "What about him, Lord?" Jesus answered, "If I want him to stay behind till I come, what does it matter to you? You are to follow me." The rumor then went out among the brothers that this disciple would not die. Yet Jesus had not said to Peter, "He will not die," but "If I want him to stay behind till I come."

In the battle between love and friendship, between the injunction to carry the Church onward and the need of even the resurrected Jesus for intimacy, it is clear that what Peter apparently suspects is actually true: that it is friendship, the incarnation of love, that endures; that it is friendship that is eternal; and that even if John will die, Jesus' love for John will not. As an image of friendship, it is hard to counter this one. Not simply the natural, instinctive resting of John's head on Jesus' chest, but the picture the Gospel gives us of the quiet, undemonstrative figure of the disciple Jesus loved, following Jesus some way behind Peter, his love not needing to be spoken, his loyalty not needing to be proved, his own Gospel a fitting and unique testimony to his own dead friend, and to the faith that, ultimately, his friend still lives.

THE DAY OF THE FUNERAL was a typically muggy one in Patrick's hometown. Our mutual friend Alane and I had gotten up before dawn in New York to make the journey down, and in Atlanta, we'd picked up the rest of his close friends for the final leg home. By the time we arrived at the spacious family house Pat had grown up in, we were ragged at the edges and still in a kind of emotional haze. Those few days since his death had been black ones, tenuous, strung-out affairs, places without many recognizable refuges and no discernible meaning. But the numbness lifted during the short car ride to the small-town church, past rows of neighbors on the streets, and bustling silence in the crammed pews. Pat's high school portrait was propped up on the altar, an airbrushed oil work that seemed as unreal as his death. So strange to be where he had taken us but, for the first time, without him; so strange to feel the eyes of a small town bear down on the huddle of suited "special friends" who had come to pay their respects.

And after the wake, his family took us down to the boat. It was late afternoon, and we were doing what he'd asked of us. There were five friends on the boat, and Pat's parents, three brothers, and their wives. We brought the ashes with us, some poems to read out loud, a trumpet to play a strain from Mahler, and, of course, some food. We knew where we were going but dreaded the moment when the boat's engine would stop, and we would be floating there in silence, above the warm, dark gulf of Sharks' Hole, waiting at last to say goodbye. I must have imagined a scene like this a dozen times over the previous few years, but it seemed even heavier than I anticipated, even emptier than I had feared. Still, there was something about the warm, gentle air that evening, and the red, incandescent sky, that leavened the atmosphere. So when the time came to empty the ashes into the still water, it was easy to be distracted by how white they were, like powdered sugar, and how they billowed so swiftly out behind the boat into the bay. We all stood there, watching the white cloud spread beneath us, wondering what to do next, when one of Pat's brothers started to take his shirt off. "I'm going in!" he yelled, and jumped in after Pat. The rest of us hesitated for a moment, and then followed.

I remember the shock of warmth as my body fell into the sea, and the strange gray mist that surrounded me as I opened my eyes in the water, and the pure, sweet breeze that greeted me as I reached the surface, and looked around me again, and breathed, suddenly, for air.

SELECT BIBLIOGRAPHY

THE FOLLOWING works are either quoted in the text or helped inform and deepen its arguments:

Aelred of Rievaulx. *Spiritual Friendship*. Translated by Mary Eugenia Laker, SSND. Kalamazoo, Mich.: Cistercian Publications, 1974.

Ariès, Philippe. *Western Attitudes Toward Death*. Translated by Patricia Ranum. Baltimore, Md.: Johns Hopkins University Press, 1974.

Aristotle. *Nicomachean Ethics*. Translated by Martin Oswald. Indianapolis: Bobbs-Merrill/Library of Liberal Arts, 1962.

Auden, W. H. *Collected Poems*. New York: Vintage, 1991.

Augustine of Hippo. *Confessions*. Translated by Henry Chadwick. New York: Oxford University Press, 1992.

Bayer, Ronald. *Homosexuality and American Psychiatry: The Politics of Diagnosis*. Princeton, N.J.: Princeton University Press, 1987.

Bem, Daryl J. "Exotic Becomes Erotic: A Developmental Theory of Sexual Orientation." *Psychological Review* 103, no. 2 (1996).

Bloom, Allan. *Love and Friendship*. New York: Simon and Schuster, 1994.

Blum, Deborah. *Sex on the Brain*. New York: Viking, 1997.

Bolt, Robert. *A Man for All Seasons*. New York: Vintage Books, 1990.

Broyard, Anatole. *Intoxicated by My Illness*. New York: Fawcett Columbine Books, 1993.

Camus, Albert. *The Plague*. New York: Vintage Books, 1991.

Chauncey, George. *Gay New York: Gender, Urban Culture, and the Making of the Gay World 1890–1940*. New York: Basic Books, 1994.

Cicero. *De Amicitia*. Translated by W. A. Falconer. Cambridge/London: Loeb Classical Library/Harvard University Press, 1923.

De Cecco, John P., and Michael G. Shively, eds. *Origins of Sexuality and Homosexuality*. New York/London: Harrington Park Press, 1984.

Defoe, Daniel. *A Journal of the Plague Year*. New York: Oxford University Press, 1990.

Derrida, Jacques. *Politics of Friendship*. London/New York: Verso Books, 1997.

Emerson, Ralph Waldo. *Essays: First and Second Series*. New York: Vintage Books/Library of America, 1990.

Freud, Sigmund. *Three Essays on the Theory of Sexuality*. Translated by James Strachey. New York: Basic Books, 1976.

———. *Civilization and Its Discontents*. New York: W. W. Norton, 1989.

Friedman, Richard C. *Male Homosexuality*. New Haven, Conn.: Yale University Press, 1990.

Isay, Richard A. *Being Homosexual: Gay Men and Their Development.* New York: Avon Books, 1990.

———. *Becoming Gay: The Journey to Self-Acceptance.* New York: Pantheon Books, 1996.

The Jerusalem Bible. London: Darton, Longman and Todd, 1966.

Lewes, Kenneth. *The Psychoanalytic Theory of Male Homosexuality.* New York: Simon and Schuster, 1988.

Lewis, C. S. *The Four Loves.* New York: Harcourt Brace Jovanovich, 1991.

McClatchy, J. D. *The Rest of the Way.* New York: Alfred A. Knopf, 1992.

Montaigne, Michel de. *The Complete Essays of Montaigne.* Translated by Donald Frame. Palo Alto, Calif.: Stanford University Press, 1958.

National Association for Research and Therapy of Homosexuality. Collected Papers from the Annual Conferences, 1994, 1995, 1996.

Oakeshott, Michael. *Rationalism in Politics and Other Essays.* Indianapolis: Liberty Press, 1991.

Odets, Walt. *In the Shadow of the Epidemic: Being H IV-Negative in the Age of A I D S.* Durham, N.C.: Duke University Press, 1995.

Orwell, George. "Looking Back on the Spanish War." From *A Collection of Essays.* New York: Harcourt Brace, 1970.

Pakaluk, Michael, ed. *Other Selves: Philosophers on Friendship.* Indianapolis/Cambridge: Hackett Publishing Company, Inc., 1991.

Price, Reynolds. *A Whole New Life: An Illness and a Healing.* New York: Plume, 1995.

Rotello, Gabriel. *Sexual Ecology: A I D S and the Destiny of Gay Men.* New York: Dutton, 1997.

Satinover, Jeffrey. *Homosexuality and the Politics of Truth.* Grand Rapids, Mich.: Baker Books, 1996.

Shakespeare, William. *Romeo and Juliet.*

Socarides, Charles W. *Homosexuality: A Freedom Too Far.* Phoenix, Ariz.: Adam Margrave Books, 1995.

Tennyson, Alfred. *In Memoriam, Maud, and Other Poems.* London: Everyman, 1991.

Thoreau, Henry David. *A Week on the Concord and Merrimack Rivers.* New York: Library of America, 1985.

Woodward, C. Vann. *The Strange Career of Jim Crow.* New York: Oxford University Press, 1974.

PERMISSIONS ACKNOWLEDGMENTS

GRATEFUL ACKNOWLEDGMENT is made to the following for permission to reprint previously published material:

BasicBooks and *The Hogarth Press:* Letter from *The Life and Work of Sigmund Freud, Vol. 3, The Last Phase 1919-1939* by Ernest Jones, copyright © 1957 by Ernest Jones, copyright renewed 1985 by Mervyn Jones. Rights outside the United States administered by The Hogarth Press, London. Reprinted by permission of BasicBooks, a subsidiary of Perseus Books Group, LLC., and The Hogarth Press. Excerpts from *Three Essays on the Theory of Sexuality* by Sigmund Freud, copyright © 1962 by Sigmund Freud Copyrights, Ltd. Rights outside the United States from *The Standard Edition of the Complete Psychological Works of Sigmund Freud,* translated and edited by James Strachey, administered by The Hogarth Press, London. Reprinted by permission of BasicBooks, a subsidiary of Perseus Books Group, LLC., and the Sigmund Freud Copyrights, The Institute of Psycho-Analysis and The Hogarth Press.

Cistercian Publications: Excerpts from *Spiritual Friendship* by Aelred of Rievaulx, translated by Mary Eugenia Laker, copyright © 1974 by Cistercian Publications. Reprinted by permission of Cistercian Publications, Kalamazoo, MI.

Farrar, Straus & Giroux, Inc., and *Faber and Faber Limited:* Excerpt from "This Be the Verse" from *Collected Poems* by Philip Larkin, copyright ©1988, 1989 by the Estate of Philip Larkin. Rights in Canada administered by Faber and Faber Limited, London. Reprinted by permission of Farrar, Straus & Giroux, Inc., and Faber and Faber Limited.

Alfred A. Knopf, Inc.: Excerpt from "An Essay on Friendship" from *The Rest of the Way* by J. D. McClatchy, copyright © 1990 by J. D. McClatchy. Reprinted by permission of Alfred A. Knopf, Inc.

Hal Leonard Corporation: Excerpt from "Left to My Own Devices," words and music by Christopher Lowe and Neil Tennant, copyright © 1988 by EMI 10 Music Ltd. and Cage Music Ltd. All rights for the U.S. and Canada controlled and administered by EMI Virgin Music, Inc. All rights reserved. International copyright secured. Reprinted by permission of Hal Leonard Corporation.

NARTH: Excerpts from "The Treatment of Egodystonic Homosexuality: The Development of a Masculine Self-Image" by Steven Richfield, Psy.D., from "Collected Papers," NARTH Annual Spring Conference, May 22, 1994; excerpts from "Coming Out of the Closet: Why I Decided

A NOTE ABOUT THE AUTHOR

ANDREW SULLIVAN is a senior editor of *The New Republic,* a contributing writer to the *New York Times Magazine,* and a columnist for *The Sunday Times* (London). From 1991 to 1996, he was editor of *The New Republic.* He holds a B.A. in modern history and modern languages from Oxford University and a Ph.D. in political science from Harvard University. He is the author of *Virtually Normal: An Argument About Homosexuality* and many articles on social and political issues, and is the editor of *Same-Sex Marriage: Pro and Con.* He lives in Washington, D.C.

A NOTE ON THE TYPE

THIS BOOK was set in Swift, a contemporary text typeface created by Dutch designer Gerard Unger. It was originally released in 1987 and subsequently digitized by the designer to be sold privately. Based on the classical pattern, this type offers impact rather than the subtlety of its aristocratic ancestors. The stroke contrast is low, x-height high, openings wide, and set width narrow. Its forms are clean, chiseled and assertive. Its italic is one of the most successful modern interpretations of chancery form.

The display type is Formata, designed by Bernd Möllenstädt and issued by Berthold in 1984.

COMPOSED BY STRATFORD PUBLISHING SERVICES,
BRATTLEBORO, VERMONT

PRINTED AND BOUND BY R. R. DONNELLY & SONS,
HARRISONBURG, VIRGINIA

DESIGNED BY MISHA BELETSKY